This book should be essential reading for any Christian concerned about divorce. Although hard to swallow today, Gordon Wenham bases his message, "Jesus did not allow remarriage after divorce," upon years of study of ancient marriage practices and careful exegesis of the Gospel passages. He shows it was also the early church's view. As in his earlier works, he is aware of the pastoral implications, but, as an experienced biblical scholar, concentrates upon the meaning of Scripture.

ALAN MILLARD
Rankin Professor Emeritus of
Hebrew and Ancient Semitic Languages,
University of Liverpool

DIVORCE, / & / REMARRIAGE

DIVORCE, / & / REMARRIAGE

In Their Historical Setting

—

GORDON J. WENHAM

LEXHAM PRESS

Jesus, Divorce, and Remarriage: In Their Historical Setting

Lexham Press, 1313 Commercial St., Bellingham, WA 98225
LexhamPress.com

Print ISBN 9781683593287
Digital ISBN 9781683593294
Library of Congress Control Number 2019950875

Lexham Editorial: Elliot Ritzema, Jim Weaver
Cover Design: Lydia Dahl
Typesetting: Abigail Stocker, Danielle Thevenaz

CONTENTS

PREFACE

—

It is now more than forty years since my interest in Jesus' teaching on divorce and remarriage was sparked off by a debate in a Church of Ireland synod. The issue was: Should divorcees be allowed to marry in church? Listening to the debate, I felt the synod members could do with some guidance on the biblical teaching if they were to determine a scriptural approach to this issue. I therefore decided to devote the summer vacation to writing an intelligible but scholarly booklet on Jesus' teaching on divorce. However, in the course of my research on this topic, I came to the conclusion that it was not just the Synod whose views needed correction but that mine required radical revision, too.

Like most twentieth-century Protestants, I was brought up to believe that marriage was for life, but that in certain limited circumstances divorce was permissible. If the divorce was legitimate, at least one of the parties could remarry. There were long debates about what situations warranted divorce: some people limited it to the innocent party in the case of adultery; at the other end of the spectrum, others would allow both sides a divorce on much slighter grounds. But hardly ever was it supposed that divorce, as understood in the New Testament, did not entitle either party to remarry. It was also largely unknown in the circles I moved in that the early church's stance was not to permit remarriage for divorcees.

But an article comparing Matthew's account of Jesus' debate with the Pharisees with Mark's version convinced me that the conventional critical reading of these passages made Matthew a fool who contradicted himself in adjacent verses.[1] I was reluctant to accept that so gifted a literary artist as the evangelist should be guilty of such incoherence in his report of Christ's teaching on marriage. I concluded that the only way to rescue Matthew's intellectual integrity was to realize he held that Jesus did not allow remarriage after divorce. Then Matthew makes sense logically.

I reached this conclusion simply by a careful reading of the text. I was not importing my own prejudices and preconceptions. As I have already mentioned, I was brought up with the view that Jesus allowed divorce in mitigating circumstances, and that entailed permission to remarry. Close study of the Gospel texts, however, led me to conclude that this was an untenable view and that Jesus never countenanced remarriage after divorce. When, soon after reaching this conclusion, I was told by an expert in church history that this was also the view of the early church, everything fitted together neatly. Jesus, as pictured by Matthew, flatly contradicted the Jewish understanding of divorce. He did not back down when challenged first by the Pharisees and then by the disciples. He taught that after divorce neither party should remarry; thus, Jesus appeared to be stricter than even the conservative Pharisees.

In the course of the next few years, I published a number of articles exploring the exegetical implications of a no-remarriage understanding of Jesus' teaching. I also collaborated with

---

1. David R. Catchpole, "The Synoptic Divorce Material as a Traditio-Historical Problem," *Bulletin of the John Rylands Library* 57 (1974): 92–127.

Bill Heth in writing *Jesus and Divorce*.[2] That book outlined the main scholarly interpretations of Jesus' teaching as recorded in Matthew and then critiqued them. It did not incorporate some of the ideas I developed later in various articles.

Though the title of the present work sounds like *Jesus and Divorce,* it is not a new edition of that work. Rather, it integrates the conclusions of *Jesus and Divorce* with ideas published elsewhere and some new ones to present an integrated argument for the no-remarriage interpretation of Jesus' teaching. Like the former work, it is not intended to be a handbook for pastoral practice. Its conclusions undoubtedly have implications for church life and modern society, but these consequences must not be based on a literalistic appeal to the text but on a sensitive understanding of the New Testament situation, wider biblical principles, and modern social realities. Above all, one must remember that divorcees have often been deeply wounded in the process and that Jesus came "to bind up the brokenhearted" (Isa 61:1), not to rub salt in their wounds. This insight must inform every discussion of this topic. I have tried hard to practice what I preach, but apologize for wherever I have failed.

Finally, I would like to thank my brother David, daughter Mary, editor Elliot Ritzema, and former student L. Michael Morales for their help in bringing this work to a conclusion.

2. Gordon J. Wenham and William A. Heth, *Jesus and Divorce* (London: Hodder & Stoughton, 1984).

INTRODUCTION

T he topic of divorce is a most sensitive one. Those who expe-
rience it are left scarred emotionally, and their social relationships are disrupted. But it is not just the divorcing couple
who are affected: friends and relatives, especially their children, if they have them, suffer too. Wider society pays a price as
well: broken marriages vastly increase the cost of welfare and
breed a low-commitment culture where one's word is no longer
one's bond. Face-to-face with the tide of misery and bitterness
unleashed by divorce, it seems only compassionate to encourage,
or at least to allow, divorcees to have a second chance. To those
brought up in the modern era, discouraging remarriage may well
feel cruel and harsh. This feeling is likely to be intensified where
the divorced person is a close friend or relative.

This certainly makes it difficult to read the Gospel texts in an
open-minded manner if we believe in their authority and look
to them to guide our behavior. In many areas of life, including
marriage, we do not want to find Christ opposing our ideas, so
we are tempted to interpret the Gospel texts in ways that do not
make us uncomfortable by disagreeing with them. This means
that we, perhaps unconsciously, interpret Christ's words to fit
our presuppositions. If we are pacifists, for example, we tend to
hold that the Sermon on the Mount teaches pacifism; but if we
have friends in the armed services, we tend to argue that Jesus

did not teach pacifism, for to say that would condemn their choice of career. Similarly, Jesus' teaching on wealth is unwelcome in our consumer society. By the standard of first-century Christians, middle-class Westerners are very wealthy, and Jesus warned that the rich would only enter the kingdom with great difficulty. The same sort of bias operates when we approach Jesus' words on marriage and divorce: we are in constant danger of reading the sayings in ways that fit our own prejudices and circumstances. By "our circumstances" I do not mean just our own marital situation but that of our family members and close friends as well.

Modern hermeneutics has taught us that it is impossible to read any text in a totally detached and objective manner. The reader always contributes to the interpretative process, sometimes positively by filling gaps and sometimes negatively by introducing ideas that are foreign to the text. Seen in this light, the danger of misreading the Gospel divorce texts is obvious. We want Jesus to be on our side and to teach what we believe; consequently, we create a Christ in our own image. This hermeneutical problem has been likened to someone looking down a well and seeing a reflection of his own face but supposing it belongs to someone else.[1] But how do we avoid this danger of looking into the past and finding ourselves there rather than the authentic Christ?

Jesus was speaking to people who were very familiar with marriage and its associated customs. If only we could recover their assumptions and background knowledge, we could interpret the teaching of Jesus with a much higher degree of confidence. Sadly, this is impossible: we are separated by two thousand years of history and immense social changes. But scholars do

---

1. Gordon J. Wenham, "The Face at the Bottom of the Well," in *He Swore an Oath: Biblical Themes from Genesis 12–50*, ed. Richard S. Hess, Gordon J. Wenham, and Philip E. Satterthwaite, 2nd ed. (Grand Rapids: Baker, 1994), 185–209.

their best to recreate the assumptions of ancient authors and readers by drawing on all we know about marriage and divorce in the ancient world. Closest to the Gospels' world of thought is, of course, Jewish law and custom. However, this was not a unity; there were different schools of thought in their approach to marriage and divorce. From the strict Essenes to the liberal Hillelites, they all claimed to be expounding the Old Testament faithfully. If understanding Jewish law is a prerequisite to understanding the New Testament, an understanding of the Old Testament is essential for understanding Jewish law, and finally a grasp of ancient Near Eastern marriage law is vital to understanding Old Testament rules. This is why we venture to explore these areas, which at first glance would seem to have nothing to do with the Gospels. It is my hope that dipping into this background material will enable us to see past our twenty-first century assumptions and get closer to how Jesus was understood by his contemporaries—and, of course, what he meant by his teaching.

As mentioned above, the goal of this book is to discover what Jesus was saying to first-century Jews about marriage and what his first-century hearers understood by his teaching. This book is not about what his teaching means today for the church and for individual Christians. It does, of course, have major implications for all those who want to be Christ's disciples, but applying his teaching to today's issues is beyond the scope of this work. This book is essentially an exercise in exegesis, drawing out the original sense the passages would have had for first-century believers. It is not an exposition that would both give the original meaning of the text and seek to apply it to today's issues. This is not a pastoral handbook; I see it rather as an essay in biblical interpretation.

1.
THE WORLD
OF THE BIBLE

At first blush, it is curious to begin a book on the teaching of Jesus by looking at the social customs of societies that were neither biblical nor contemporary with him. Yet this is what I propose to do. This is because these ancient societies were much closer to the biblical pattern of life than ours is. Also, their basic social structures survived at least into the first millennium BC and, in slightly modified form, into the Christian era. So when we try to understand the Gospels and find gaps in our knowledge, we shall be on much safer ground if we fill these gaps by appealing to ancient custom than by filling them by guesswork based on modern practice.

There are many ways in which traditional societies differ from modern society.[1] There are the obvious technological revolutions, such as advances in agriculture, medicine, transport, and electronics that have transformed life for many people. But it is not computers, TV, motor vehicles, and aircraft that have changed daily life most fundamentally so much as the way modern society is structured. To put it over-simply: in traditional societies (this would also apply to many modern-day Eastern cultures), the community is fundamental, whereas in Western society the individual is all-important. Your place in modern society is determined by your education, innate ability, and job opportunities, but in traditional society, it is birth that determines where you live and your occupation. For example, you could become a priest

---

1. For a fuller discussion, see Roland de Vaux, *Ancient Israel: Its Life and Institutions* (London: Darton, Longman, & Todd, 1962); and Richard S. Hess and M. Daniel Carroll R., *Family in the Bible: Exploring Customs, Culture, and Context* (Grand Rapids: Baker Academic, 2003).

in Jerusalem because your father was a priest and his father was a priest before him. But if you were not the son of a priest, you could never become one. Quite different are the criteria for becoming a Christian minister: after an assessment of your suitability for the role, you become a Christian pastor or priest through training at seminary and then by working with an older minister. In Britain, the royal family is one of the few relics of traditional social organization that survives. You cannot become king of England by taking a degree in royalty studies! You must be the queen's son.

These different social structures have an important effect on the approach to marriage. In traditional societies, marriage involves the union of two tribes or families, whereas in today's society it is seen essentially as a link-up of two individuals: the implications of their alliance for society as a whole tend to be regarded as of little importance. These different attitudes to society and marriage customs must be borne in mind throughout the following review of marriage and divorce down through the centuries. From the Patriarchs in the early second millennium BC to the Jews in the first century AD, the fundamental assumptions about family were very different from ours. This is why this study begins with a look at the non-biblical setting of ancient matrimony.

MARRIAGE IN THE ANCIENT WORLD

For our purposes, the best sources of information are texts from the Old Babylonian period, roughly 2000 to 1600 BC, when the first dynasty of Babylon was the dominant power in the ancient Near East. The most famous king of this dynasty was Hammurabi (1792–1750). We have two law codes from this era (the Code of Hammurabi, c. 1750 BC; and the Code of Eshnunna, c. 1770 BC),

which show how the Babylonians sought to structure society.[2]
We also have thousands of legal texts, including ninety marriage
documents describing how they did in fact operate.[3] I shall therefore draw heavily on Old Babylonian texts to develop a picture of
ancient Near Eastern marriage.[4]

Biblical narratives are another rich source. One of the most
informative passages about the preliminaries to marriage is
found in Genesis 24, which tells how Abraham's servant was sent
by Abraham to find a wife for his son Isaac.

In biblical times, marriages were frequently arranged for the
bride and groom by their parents. Genesis 24 tells how the marriage of Isaac and Rebekah was organized without the couple
even meeting, nor were the parents of Isaac and Rebekah directly
involved. Abraham's servant did the negotiations on his master's
behalf. That such a marriage was divinely approved is grudgingly
admitted by Laban and Bethuel, who say, "The thing has come
from the LORD" (Gen 24:50). Isaac did not say or do anything
until Rebekah arrived at Abraham's camp. Rebekah's opinion was
not sought until all the negotiations had been completed and the
servant was ready to return to Abraham.

The fullness of this account shows its importance and suggests
the story was probably used to inculcate the virtue of arranged
marriage. It certainly shows how marriage was viewed not as a
private arrangement between two individuals but as something
that involved the extended family and potentially the larger clan.
The substance of the negotiations is only alluded to in Genesis,

---

2. Edited and translated in Martha T. Roth, *Law Collections from Mesopotamia
and Asia Minor*, 2nd ed., Writings from the Ancient World 6 (Atlanta: Scholars
Press, 1997), 57–142.

3. Raymond Westbrook, *Old Babylonian Marriage Law* (Horn, Austria: Verlag
Ferdinand Berger & Söhne, 1988), 2.

4. For a detailed analysis, see Westbrook, *Old Babylonian Marriage Law*.

and it is here that the Old Babylonian texts are so helpful. From them we learn that a payment was made to mark the agreement to marry. This sum of money, best called the bride-money, was given by the groom's family to the bride's family. Because it looked as though the groom was buying the bride, the bride-money has sometimes been called the bride price. But this is not accurate. What the bride-money did was transfer authority over the bride from her parents to the groom's family.[5] In Old Babylonian times, the bride-money varied between one and forty shekels, a substantial sum when a laborer was paid a shekel a month.[6] This payment effected betrothal or, more precisely, inchoate marriage, for the bride was now regarded as her husband's wife. Although she still lived in her father's house, any intercourse with her by a third party counted as adultery.[7] The same rule applied in the land of Israel some centuries later (Deut 22:23–26).

The payment of bride-money was a pledge that both parties would fulfill all the regular procedures to complete the marriage union. If the bride's family subsequently pulled out of the commitment, they forfeited the bride-money given to them by the groom's father. If it was the groom's family that reneged on the agreement, they forfeited the bride-money plus an equal sum. Thus the penalty for withdrawal from the match was the same for both parties. Given the size of the bride-money, there was a strong incentive to go through with the marriage. Its payment signaled that the bride's parents were relinquishing their authority over her and were ready to allow her to move from their home to the groom's abode. This move was the central part of the wedding

---

5. For detailed discussion, see Westbrook, *Old Babylonian Marriage Law*, 58–60.

6. A laborer or craftsman was paid about a shekel a month according to Code of Hammurabi 273–74.

7. Code of Eshnunna 26, 28.

ceremony, but there were, of course, many other customary acts, notably a wedding breakfast lasting several days, a recital of the wedding contract, and probably an exchange of pledges along the lines of: "You, X, are now my wife." To which the bride replied: "You, Y, are now my husband." It was probably at this time that the dowry was given to the bride. The dowry was a gift to the bride from her father.[8]

There were doubtless many other customs that the ancients were familiar with but had no need to specify because they were taken for granted. But the giving of the dowry was very important and is often detailed in wedding contracts. Essentially, the dowry was a large present from the bride's father to the bride. Typically, it contained clothing, jewelry, kitchen utensils, furniture, and sometimes slaves, livestock, and land, but not money.[9] Though legally the dowry belonged to the bride, in practice it was managed by the husband. However, if the marriage was terminated by death or divorce, its ownership by the wife became very significant since the dowry acted as an endowment if the wife was widowed and as a divorce settlement if she was divorced.[10] For this reason, the dowry's content was carefully recorded as it had to be preserved intact in case the widowed or divorced wife needed to take it with her.

DIVORCE IN THE ANCIENT WORLD

As already mentioned, the dowry played an important role in divorce. The fate of the dowry in divorce proceedings depended on the reason for the divorce. If the wife was innocent of any unfaithfulness and had borne some children for her husband,

---

8. A full discussion can be found in Westbrook, *Old Babylonian Marriage Law*, 48–60.

9. Westbrook, *Old Babylonian Marriage Law*, 90.

10. Westbrook, *Old Babylonian Marriage Law*, 91–94.

she retained the dowry in full, in fact in its original condition. Her husband had to make good for any wear and tear. In addition, she might receive a divorce payment. If, on the other hand, she was guilty of some marital offense short of adultery, her husband could withhold some or all of the dowry, depending on the nature of the offense.

In principle, it was quite easy for a man to divorce his wife. All he had to do was to say "you are not my wife" in the presence of his wife and some witnesses. Divorce was an essentially private procedure. No appearance in court was required for the divorce itself,[11] though it might be required if there were disputes about property.

Thus the divorce ceremony was quite simple and could be invoked for any reason,[12] but this did not mean that divorces were frequent. This was due to the heavy costs involved in many situations, which would deter couples from resorting to divorce. For example, if a man divorced his childless wife without good reason, he must give her a sum equal to the bride-money and refund her dowry. If she was married without payment of the bride-money, he must pay sixty shekels and refund her dowry.[13] But if his wife had borne him children and he took another wife, he would forfeit his house and all his property.[14] If, however, the wife had misbehaved, her husband could divorce her without cost. If she and her lover were caught in the act of adultery, they could be put to death. If the aggrieved husband wished to spare his wife, her

---

11.   Westbrook, *Old Babylonian Marriage Law*, 69.

12.   There is no evidence that divorce "for any cause" was an innovation of the Pharisees as David Instone-Brewer has argued in *Divorce and Remarriage in the Bible* (Grand Rapids: Eerdmans, 2002), 43–47.

13.   Code of Hammurabi 138–39.

14.   Code of Eshnunna 59.

lover must be spared too.[15] In this case and other serious offenses, the wife could be divorced without any compensation or refund of her dowry.[16]

It has been argued that a wife had no right to divorce her husband, but this has been refuted by Raymond Westbrook.[17] As with the husband, it seems likely that a wife could initiate a divorce by saying something similar to "You are not my husband." However, divorce was not to be undertaken lightly by a woman, for there were heavy penalties for invoking that right without strong evidence of her husband's misconduct. A would-be divorcee seeking a divorce without good grounds could face the death penalty by drowning or by being thrown from a tower (defenestration), or she could face heavy financial penalties.

The general picture that emerges from these Old Babylonian texts is that marriage was taken very seriously since it represents the union of two families. The heads of the family have more say in arranging the match than the couple involved. This is partly a consequence of the couple's ages: they would mostly be teenagers just past puberty. It was also necessitated by the large financial payments associated with marriage and divorce, such as the dowry and bride-money. In modern terms, these represented large capital transfers between the families involved. Divorce, as I have said, was quite a simple procedure, merely requiring the utterance, "You are not my wife/husband," but the costs involved must have been a strong deterrent to seeking divorce unless there were very good grounds.[18]

15. Code of Eshnunna 28; Code of Hammurabi 129.

16. Westbrook, *Old Babylonian Marriage Law,* 75–76.

17. Westbrook, *Old Babylonian Marriage Law,* 80–83.

18. A twentieth-century survey in Arab Palestinian villages found a divorce rate of about 5 percent thanks to the necessity of returning the dowry. See Hilma

POLYGAMY IN THE ANCIENT WORLD

Some of the Old Babylonian marriage contracts mention the possibility of the husband taking a second wife. These documents seek to regulate relations between the two wives and between the wives and the husband. Various situations are envisaged. The wives may be sisters and their father decided to marry them both off to the same man. Or the first wife may have had a slave-girl as part of her dowry so that when the woman married, the slave-girl became the man's second wife. At the same time, she remained the property of the first wife.

Another reason for polygamy was childlessness, seen as a disaster in the ancient world. Both affection for his first wife and the cost of divorce could prompt a husband not to divorce her but to take a second wife in the hope of acquiring an heir. A further motive for taking a second wife was incurable sickness in the first wife. Yet another reason would be to punish a first wife for misconduct short of adultery. She could be divorced without compensation or she could be reduced to the status of slave wife in her husband's home.

Whatever the reason for taking a second wife, there were doubtless plenty of complications. Nevertheless, the high cost of divorce, with its requirement of returning the dowry if the first wife had not misbehaved, probably limited the number of marriages in which the husband took a second wife.

SUMMARY

This review of marriage law and custom in the Old Babylonian era has disclosed a very different approach to these issues from modern Western social attitudes and customs. Of course, quite

---

Granquist, *Marriage Conditions in a Palestinian Village, vol. II* (Helsingfors: Akademische Buchhandlung, 1935), 271, 284.

similar attitudes to marriage survive in traditional societies today. But in our society, relations between the sexes have become quite fluid and individualistic. Many couples live together without even a wedding ceremony, let alone obtaining their parents' agreement to the union. The decision to marry or to live together is seen to be the concern of the individuals involved; other people's opinion does not really matter.

The high value attached to marriage in traditional society had as its counterpart the horror of singleness. To be single implied that one would be childless in later life, and this for a woman was tragic (see Rachel, Hannah, and Elizabeth in Gen 30:1; 1 Sam 1:2–11; Luke 1:7). Without children, you would have no one to care for you in old age or to tend your grave. For similar reasons, the plight of eunuchs who did not or could not marry and father children was regarded as pitiable and to be avoided at all costs (Isa 56:3–5). To lose one's ability to become a parent was seen as catastrophic, but singleness attracted little sympathy, and in the case of divorce imposed for adultery it was doubtless treated with scorn. By contrast, in modern society—and indeed in Paul's first letter to the Corinthians—the single life is not regarded as necessarily inferior to marriage.

Similarly, divorce in the modern West is seen as essentially the concern of the couple: the implications of the break-up for the children, if there are any, and relatives and friends of the divorcing couple are seen as relatively unimportant. In Western society, the insignificance of divorce compared with other rites of passage, such as weddings and funerals, is signaled by the minimal amount of ritual associated with divorce. Unions between the sexes can be characterized as "easy come, easy go." This is most evident where couples move in together without being married, but the approach also influences traditional marriage to some extent. Whatever the wedding vows say, many do not think that they apply "till death us do part."

Very different was the attitude in Bible times. Though in Babylon and Israel they did not hold to the indissolubility of marriage, the social ramifications of marriage and divorce made it very difficult to walk out of a Babylonian marriage. I have noted the father's role in the pre-marriage negotiations, which could begin well before the potential bride and groom were of age. These negotiations involved agreeing on the bride-money, a hefty payment often amounting to several years' pay, and the marriage had to be authorized by the head of the family, not just the happy couple. Should the marriage prove to be less than happy, it was no easy matter to escape. Divorce could be initiated by the husband or the wife, and all it required was for the man or wife to declare "you are not my wife/husband" and the divorce was effected. A divorce for any cause was always possible.[19] However, the financial implications of divorce were such that unless the husband was the gravely injured party, he would stand to forfeit the valuable dowry. Sometimes part or all of the bride-money would also have to be repaid: the penalties could vary. A woman who sued for divorce could be the subject of a counter claim by her husband, which, if upheld, would spell her financial ruin and even cost her life in some cases.

These provisions attest to the seriousness with which marriage was viewed in second-millennium BC society. It was not something that the individual could walk into or out of whenever he or she liked: it concerned the whole family, especially its head. In its general ethos, as well as in its detailed provisions, the

---

19. David W. Amram, *The Jewish Law of Divorce according to Bible and Talmud with Some Reference to Its Development in Post-Talmudic Times* (1896; repr. New York: Hermon Press, 1975), 22–31.

Old Babylonian approach to marriage differed fundamentally from modern attitudes and law. However, it has many features in common with the laws and customs enshrined in the Pentateuch, which we shall look at next.

2.

MARRIAGE AND DIVORCE IN THE OLD TESTAMENT

Despite the size of the Old Testament, it is not easy to write a history of marriage in ancient Israel. There are two main reasons for this. First, knowledge of marriage law and customs is often presupposed by the writers and therefore these customs are left unexplained. This requires modern interpreters to read between the lines with the help of texts from neighboring societies. This approach is warranted because, as Raymond Westbrook observes, "Biblical law was part of a much wider legal tradition that extended across the whole of the ancient Near East."[1] But although appealing to neighboring cultures reduces the amount of interpretative guesswork involved, it does not eliminate it altogether.

The other difficulty concerns the dating of the material.[2] Few scholars would doubt that the entire Old Testament was written between 1300 and 150 BC, but the date of a book or part of a book is more contentious, especially the Pentateuch, which is the most informative text for understanding marriage. Its date of composition has been debated *ad nauseam*.

But this is not so problematic as it seems at first, since the provisions of the Pentateuch are so similar to Old Babylonian rules. And the date of composition matters little for the educative function of the biblical texts, which were designed to be recited at festive gatherings to instruct the people in how to behave. Neither reciter nor listener worried about when the text was written, only

---

1. Raymond Westbrook, *Property and the Family in Biblical Law* (Sheffield: Sheffield Academic, 1991), 11.

2. Gordon J. Wenham, *Exploring the Old Testament 1: The Pentateuch* (Downers Grove, IL: InterVarsity Press, 2003).

about its message.[3] And though the material in the Pentateuch originated in the second millennium BC, it was incorporated into the definitive history of Israel, which is constituted by the first nine books of the Old Testament, from Genesis to 2 Kings.[4] This suggests that the laws and narratives in this history were regarded as normative well into the first millennium BC. This allows us to use the laws about marriage in the books of Exodus and Deuteronomy and the stories in Genesis and Samuel to illuminate the theory and practice of marriage in the postexilic era (roughly 500 BC onward). We also get glimpses of how marriage worked in practice in texts of this period. The books of Nehemiah and Ezra record the trouble these leaders had trying to regulate Jewish marriages. And from Elephantine, a colony of Jews in southern Egypt, we have some fifth-century marriage contracts that also shed light on ancient practice.

MARRIAGE AND DIVORCE IN THE PATRIARCHAL ERA

Marriage figures frequently in Genesis. It is presupposed in the first command given to the human race, "Be fruitful and multiply" (Gen 1:28), a command repeated three times to Noah after the flood (Gen 8:17; 9:1, 7). The topic of marriage is central in many episodes, including Adam and Eve, Cain, Abraham and Sarah, Isaac and Rebekah, Jacob and Leah and Rachel, and Dinah (Gen 2–3; 4:17–24; 12:10–20; 20:1–18; 24:1–67; 29:1–35; 34:1–31). Some of these stories present examples of good conduct, but rather more serve as warnings showing mistakes that should not be

---

3. Paul J. Griffiths, *Religious Reading* (New York: Oxford University Press, 1999); David M. Carr, *Writing on the Tablet of the Heart* (New York: Oxford University Press, 2005).

4. See Yoram Hazony, *The Philosophy of Hebrew Scripture* (Cambridge: Cambridge University Press, 2012).

repeated. Both types of story show how marriage operated in biblical times. The initial negotiations for Rebekah's hand in marriage are described in Genesis 24, and the tricky situation created by Dinah's abduction leading to agreement under duress is told in Genesis 34.[5] In both cases, the bride's father ought to have led the discussion, but with the father's reluctance to intervene, the bride's brother(s) led the haggling (Gen 24:29–30; 34:8–24). Both scenarios illustrate how marriage was the concern of the whole family, not just the bride and groom. But Jacob's flight from home made him vulnerable when it came to marriage. He had no back-up from his family and his weakness was cruelly exploited by his uncle Laban (Gen 29:15–30).

One of the key issues in these negotiations was the amount of bride-money to be paid to effect betrothal or inchoate marriage. This payment by the groom's family was a pledge that the proposed match would be carried through. The amount of bride-money varied from family to family. In Old Babylonian texts roughly contemporary with the patriarchal period, bride-money typically ranged from one to forty shekels. So keen was Shechem to regularize his relationship to Dinah that he offered to pay "whatever you say to me" (Gen 34:12). The sums usually involved were so large, several years' pay, that the groom could not pay it out of his own pocket but depended on his family.[6] Jacob's family was too far away to help, so Jacob offered to work for Laban for seven years. This timeframe was a bit longer than

---

5. For further discussion see Robin A. Parry, *Old Testament Story and Christian Ethics: The Rape of Dinah as a Case Study* (Milton Keynes: Paternoster, 2004); Daniel Hankore, *The Abduction of Dinah: Reading Genesis 28:10–35:15 as a Votive Narrative* (Eugene, OR: Pickwick, 2013).

6. A laborer in Old Babylonian times earned about one shekel a month; see Code of Hammurabi 273–74.

usual, but that no doubt reflects Jacob's love for Rachel on the one hand and Laban's avarice on the other.

An even bigger payment in Old Babylonian society was the dowry, a gift from the bride's family to the bride as a sort of endowment in case she was widowed or divorced. There are only two explicit mentions of the dowry in the Old Testament (Exod 18:2; 1 Kgs 9:16), so it has been doubted whether it was customary in Bible times to give a dowry.[7] However, this is a rather unlikely conclusion in the light of the dowry's pervasiveness in traditional societies. Also, there are quite a few passages where the dowry is alluded to and must be assumed. In Genesis, Bilhah and Zilpah are given to Rachel and Leah by Laban when they marry (Gen 29:23–29). In non-biblical texts, slave girls are frequently listed in the dowries of wealthy women. The status of Hagar and Rebekah's maids is not so clear, but it is quite likely that they were given to Sarah and Rebekah at their weddings.[8] The picture that emerges of marriage in Genesis is thus very similar to that in Old Babylonian documents.

A similar conclusion is to be drawn about polygamy. Both the Old Testament and Old Babylonian texts allow for polygamy, although both are rather uncomfortable with it. Polygamists are portrayed in the Old Testament as rather unsavory characters and their marriages are unhappy affairs (Gen 4:23–24; Gen 29–30; 1 Sam 1:1–20). This fits the general picture that marriage and its associated customs in the Old Testament were similar to those in Old Babylonia.

Further support is provided by a comparison of the laws dealing with marital offenses. In both societies, adultery was a most

---

7. Roland de Vaux, *Ancient Israel* (London: Darton, Longman & Todd, 1962), 28.

8. Westbrook, *Property and the Family,* 142–64.

serious offense for which the aggrieved husband could demand the death penalty.[9] Note that adultery is understood as intercourse by a married woman with a man who is not her husband, and the same rule applies to inchoately married (betrothed) women (Deut 22:23–24). In traditional cultures, a married man was not regarded as guilty of adultery if he had sexual intercourse with an unmarried girl. If caught red-handed, both the unfaithful wife and her lover were liable to the death penalty (Lev 20:10; Deut 22:22; compare Code of Hammurabi 129; Middle Assyrian Laws 13). The injured husband could decide to spare his wife, and in that case her lover had to be spared too. Both biblical and extrabiblical codes insist that both parties must be treated the same. This ensures that an innocent man cannot be framed, as with Joseph and Potiphar's wife in Genesis 39 (see also Code of Hammurabi 129). Both legal systems distinguish rape from seduction by appealing to the place where the offense occurred. If the assault occurred in the open country out of earshot of other people who might have heard the woman's cry for help, only the man was blamed and punished. But if it took place indoors, the woman was deemed to have consented, so both were punished (Deut 22:25–27; compare Code of Hammurabi 130; Middle Assyrian Laws 13).

The laws we have looked at cover a range of offenses where the guilt or innocence of those involved is clear. It should be noted that in Israel, as in neighboring societies, the penalty prescribed is the maximum allowed: where the death penalty is authorized the offended party may waive it if he sees fit. Proverbs 6:31–35 warns the would-be adulterer not to count on the angry husband letting him off. This shows that the death penalty did not have to

---

9. Compare William L. Moran, "The Scandal of the 'Great Sin' at Ugarit," *Journal of Near Eastern Studies* 18 (1959): 280–81.

be enforced. It seems likely, therefore, that in Israel as elsewhere in the ancient Near East death was the maximum, not the minimum, penalty for adultery. Does this mean that if the husband exercises mercy, his unfaithful wife gets away scot free and continues to live with him as though nothing had happened and the co-respondent does not suffer for his offense? This seems unlikely, as the book of Proverbs says:

> If he is caught, he will pay sevenfold; he will give all the goods of his house. (Prov 6:31)

> For jealousy makes a man furious, and he will not spare when he takes revenge. (Prov 6:34)

And the unfaithful wife is likely to have had to pay, too. Husbands could divorce their wives at any time, and would most likely want to exercise that option if their wife had misbehaved. The husband's desire for revenge would also be encouraged by the consideration that the wife would forfeit her dowry in these circumstances.

However, if a husband divorced his wife on lesser grounds, she retained her dowry and the husband who had been using it while the marriage survived had to give it back intact. This would have acted as a disincentive to divorce on trivial grounds. At least, this is how a divorce settlement might have worked in Babylon in the days of the Patriarchs. But one biblical law on divorce seems to imply similar considerations operated in Israel. Deuteronomy 24:1–4 reads:

> When a man takes a wife and marries her, if then she finds no favor in his eyes because he has found some indecency in her, and he writes her a certificate of divorce and puts it in her hand and sends her out of his house, and she departs

out of his house, and if she goes and becomes another man's wife, and the latter man hates her and writes her a certificate of divorce and puts it in her hand and sends her out of his house, or if the latter man dies, who took her to be his wife, then her former husband, who sent her away, may not take her again to be his wife, after she has been defiled, for that is an abomination before the LORD. And you shall not bring sin upon the land that the LORD your God is giving you for an inheritance.

This law falls into two main sections: verses 1–3 are background and give interesting insights into the operation of divorce in Israel, but these verses are not trying to regulate procedures. The regulation is in verse 4, which forbids a divorced woman returning to her first husband if her second husband divorces her or dies.

What is the reason for this ban? This question has perplexed commentators down through the centuries. Would such a renewal of the previous marriage look as though adultery were being tacitly endorsed?[10] Or is it regarded as a sort of incest?[11] Neither explanation is plausible.[12] But if one takes into account the financial consequences of divorce under different circumstances in the ancient Near East, a convincing explanation emerges. If a woman is divorced for immoral conduct short of adultery, she forfeits the dowry that she brought into the marriage: her husband keeps it to his financial advantage. If, on the other hand, a

---

10. So, for example, Peter C. Craigie, *Deuteronomy,* 2nd ed., New International Commentary on the Old Testament (Grand Rapids: Eerdmans, 1976). Compare C. F. Keil and Franz Delitzsch, *Biblical Commentary on the Old Testament, vol. III,* reprint ed. (Grand Rapids: Eerdmans, 1988), 418.

11. So Reuven Yaron, "The Restoration of Marriage," *Journal of Jewish Studies* 17 (1966): 1–11; Gordon J. Wenham, "The Restoration of Marriage Reconsidered," *Journal of Jewish Studies* 30 (1979): 36–40.

12. Westbrook, *Property and the Family.*

woman is divorced merely because her husband dislikes her, he
can still divorce her but she keeps her dowry in its entirety and
her husband loses the use of it. This would surely make the husband think again about divorce.

If we apply this logic to the case described in Deuteronomy
24:1–4, then the woman in verse 1 is divorced for allegedly
immoral conduct. The Hebrew translated "some indecency" is
erwath davar, literally "nakedness of a thing." It is not clear what
is referred to, but it is generally held to be some kind of sexual
immorality less serious than adultery, for which the death penalty is mandated.[13] As a result, she moves out of her marital home
without her dowry, which her first husband now owns outright:
"because he has found some indecency in her, and he writes her
a certificate of divorce and puts it in her hand and sends her out
of his house."

Then, in verse 2, she remarries and her family provides a
second dowry for her to take into her new relationship. But this
second marriage does not last long: her new husband dies or
divorces her for a minor offense (see verse 3). Her second husband dies or divorces her because he "hates" her; that is, he dislikes her and does not want to live with her, although she has not
done anything to shame him publicly. Divorce on these grounds
means that the woman leaves her second husband's home, but
this time she takes her dowry with her. She would also keep her
dowry if her husband died. As owner of a substantial dowry, she
becomes a target for predatory males, including her first husband.

---

13.   See Gordon P. Hugenberger, *Marriage as a Covenant: Biblical Law
and Ethics as Developed from Malachi,* Supplements to Vetus Testamentum
52 (Leiden: Brill, 1994), 78–81. It might perhaps cover adultery in cases where
the husband spares his wife. Whatever the precise situation, it is clear that
Deuteronomy 24, like Old Babylonian law many centuries earlier, discriminates
between divorce for sexual misbehavior and divorce for aversion by making the
latter much more costly.

If her first husband marries her again, he will gain control of her second dowry. This is clearly sharp practice. Indeed, Deuteronomy brands it an "abomination" bringing sin upon the holy land (verse 4). It is obviously a very underhanded method of making money and an unscrupulous use of divorce proceedings. The first husband demonstrates that his original charge against his wife of serious immorality, "some indecency," was only a ploy to acquire her dowry. Her innocence is demonstrated by his keenness to remarry her. Not only does he want to enrich himself on the back of false accusation, but these lies must have put his wife and her family to public shame. It is an abuse of divorce rules in which he has doubtless perjured himself by bearing false witness against his neighbor.

This interpretation of Deuteronomy 24:1–4 is straightforward and plausible. It receives independent support from its position in the book of Deuteronomy. Chapters 12–26 are often called the Code of Deuteronomy, as they systematically organize the individual laws in the sequence of the Ten Commandments. On this basis, one might anticipate locating Deuteronomy 24:1–4 near other laws on sexual misconduct in chapter 22. Instead, it is located near other laws dealing with sharp business practices regarding such things as loans, pledges, slave-trading, and wages (23:15–24:22). We could see the collection of laws in chapter 24 as applying the principle of the eighth commandment, "You shall not steal," to the realms of law and business. Seen in this light, Deuteronomy 24:1–4 is aimed at outlawing corrupt business practices and sits very comfortably where it does among other laws on this theme.

This passage shows there was one approach to divorce whatever the motivation in a particular case, but that the cost of divorce varied with that motivation: the more serious the accusation, the less divorce cost the offended party, and vice versa. It also sheds light on divorce proceedings. Twice the passage mentions that the husband must write his wife a certificate of divorce and put it into her hand. This insistence on writing a certificate and putting it in the wife's hand is striking. Scholars usually suppose that it is designed to prevent the woman from being accused of adultery if she enters into a relationship with another man.[14] Deuteronomy 24 does not mention any other public ceremony to mark divorce. Old Babylonian texts mention a public declaration that effects divorce. All that the divorcing spouse had to do was say, "You are not my wife/husband," pay the appropriate penalty, and the divorce was done. It seems likely that divorce rites in Israel involved a similar declaration of which we may hear an echo in Hosea 2:2:

> Plead with your mother, plead—
>> For she is not my wife, and I am not her husband—

Hosea was preaching in the eighth century BC, some thousand years after the Old Babylonian period, and he thus bears witness to the survival of divorce principles of the early second millennium into the mid-first millennium BC.

MARRIAGE AND DIVORCE IN THE POSTEXILIC PERIOD

Were the divorce principles we have seen still current in the first century AD? It seems likely, but we must examine the evidence. Some texts from the fifth century BC are pertinent.

Ezra and Nehemiah were exiles in Babylon who, apparently independently, returned to Jerusalem and instituted reforms

---

14. See Jeffrey H. Tigay, *Deuteronomy*, The JPS Torah Commentary (Philadelphia: Jewish Publication Society, 1996), 222; Christopher J. H. Wright, *Deuteronomy*, Understanding the Bible Commentary Series (Grand Rapids: Baker Books, 2012), 255.

there. Ezra, a priest, prefaced his demands for reform by hold-ing a public reading of the law, probably the whole Pentateuch.[15] Various issues that were raised by the law but were not being taken seriously by the people are highlighted, including Sabbath observance, the celebration of the festivals, support of temple worship, and so on (see Ezra 8–10; Neh 8–10, 13). But time and again, Ezra and Nehemiah return to the problem of mixed mar-riage, something strictly forbidden in Deuteronomy 7: "You shall make no covenant with them and show no mercy to them. You shall not intermarry with them, giving your daughters to their sons or taking their daughters for your sons" (Deut 7:2–3).

In its original context, this command applies to the indige-nous inhabitants of Canaan and reflects a fear that such unions will lead Israel into adopting Canaanite beliefs and worship. Ezra and Nehemiah apply this principle to the marriages between Jews and their neighbors: "We have broken faith with our God and have married foreign women from the peoples of the land" (Ezra 10:2; compare Neh 13:23–29). Ezra, therefore, introduced a covenant for the assent of all the people: they swore an oath to divorce their foreign wives (Ezra 10:5). Those involved came from all strata of society: priests, Levites, singers, and ordinary people (Ezra 10). It may be that these mixed marriages were viewed as not true marriage or that they constituted "some indecency" (Deut 24:1).[16] The issue was more of faith and less of ethnicity, as foreigners who professed faith in Yahweh could intermarry with Israel (for example, Rahab and Ruth). It seems likely, then, that these postexilic marriages to pagan women were considered

---

15. So Hugh G. M. Williamson, *Ezra, Nehemiah,* Word Biblical Commentary (Waco: Word Books, 1985), xxxviii–xxxix.

16. Compare Williamson *Ezra, Nehemiah,* 150–56.

rebellious and invalid by Nehemiah, who understood Israel's history of apostasy through intermarriage with pagan spouses.[17]

The New Testament will similarly call Christians not to be "yoked with unbelievers" (2 Cor 6:14), yet Paul will also instruct Christians who were converted after marriage to maintain their marital relationships with unbelieving spouses in the hope of their salvation (1 Cor 7:13–16). While there are many questions raised by Ezra and Nehemiah's drastic stance, it at least shows the authority they ascribed to Pentateuchal law, not least in the areas of marriage and divorce.

A similar attitude emerges from Ezra's near-contemporary, the prophet Malachi. His short prophecy is pervaded by allusions to the Pentateuch, especially the book of Deuteronomy. This is further evidence of the authority of the law in the preaching of the postexilic community.[18] Most interesting is Malachi's apparent appeal to the divorce law in Deuteronomy 24 (Mal 2:10–16).

These verses are exceptionally difficult to translate.[19] Traditionally, verse 16's opening words are translated, "For I hate divorce, says the LORD" (RSV), but Hugenberger has plausibly argued that we have here a reference to divorce based purely on aversion ("hate," "not love") as opposed to divorce prompted by infidelity or similar behavior. Divorce based on mere dislike is condemned as "covering one's garment with violence" (2:16 RSV). "For the man who does not love his wife but divorces her, says the LORD, the God of Israel, covers his garment with violence, says the LORD of hosts. So guard yourselves in your spirit, and do not

---

17. J. Daniel Hays, *From Every People and Nation: A Biblical Theology of Race* (Downers Grove, IL: InterVarsity Press, 2003), 78–79.

18. See Hugenberger, *Marriage as a Covenant*, 18–20.

19. For the most thorough discussion, see Hugenberger, *Marriage as a Covenant*.

be faithless" (2:16 ESV). Quite what the garment symbolizes is problematic, most likely one's own reputation or wife.

MARRIAGE AND DIVORCE AT ELEPHANTINE

In addition to Ezra, Nehemiah, and Malachi, a third fifth-century source is a collection of documents from Jews in Egypt. Elephantine was a small garrison town in southern Egypt manned by Aramaic-speaking Jews. Most of the papyri discovered there date from the latter part of the fifth century BC. A few of the texts deal with marriage and divorce, some of which show interesting innovation in religion and legal practice.

In religion, the Elephantine Jews were syncretists and would have been damned by prophets like Jeremiah (see Jer 44) and Malachi, not to mention reformers like Ezra and Nehemiah. For example, these Egyptian Jews were prepared to invoke non-Israelite gods in blessings.

Similarly, in the laws on marriage they appear to adopt Egyptian practice at certain points.[20] But these changes in details serve only to emphasize that in broad outline marriage customs had not changed since the early second millennium BC. Marriages were still arranged by the parents for their children. The same payments, bride-money, dowry, and divorce payments were recognized as before in Babylon and Israel. Divorce payments were smaller, typically seven and a half shekels as opposed to twenty to sixty in the Code of Hammurabi. This could have made divorce easier to afford, but the need to repay the dowry would have, again, been a great disincentive to rapidly resort to divorce. Whether women had the right to initiate divorce under Old Babylonian law is controversial, and earlier I tentatively accepted the possibility

---

20. See Reuven Yaron, "Aramaic Marriage Contracts from Elephantine," *Journal of Semitic Studies* 3 (1958): 36.

that women could sue for divorce. But at Elephantine women definitely could initiate divorce—though, as earlier, it could prove risky financially. Finally, at Elephantine adultery was not a capital offense, a break with all earlier ancient Near Eastern law.

SUMMARY

I have argued that Deuteronomy 24 differentiates between divorce for sexual immorality and divorce for aversion by making the latter much more costly: the aggrieved husband forfeits the dowry that his wife brought into the marriage and he also has to compensate his wife with a divorce payment, perhaps as much as the original bride-money. But if he divorces his wife for infidelity or some other serious fault, he pays nothing and keeps the dowry, while the wife is sent away with nothing. It is not divorce based on marital misbehavior that Malachi later addresses, but divorce prompted by "hatred," aversion. Malachi underlines the divine disapproval of divorce based on mere aversion by describing it as "covering one's garment with violence" and "faithlessness."

The changes in marriage law that we see at Elephantine introduced a greater degree of reciprocity between the sexes. Both man and wife could seek redress for the other's misbehavior by obtaining a divorce, and the relative cost of divorce was reduced, probably making it more frequent. One document deals with a woman's *third* marriage. This trend to more frequent divorce, often for trivial reasons, continues in later Jewish law, to which we turn next.

3.

—

LATER JEWISH ATTITUDES TO DIVORCE

Accurate interpretation of the Gospel texts on divorce and remarriage presupposes a clear understanding of first-century Jewish teaching and practice. But the sheer quantity and diversity of Jewish materials makes arriving at a clear picture a daunting task. Few texts are exactly contemporary with the Gospels, but there are many from the preceding and subsequent eras. As observed in the last chapter, from the fifth century BC we have a group of letters and legal documents from Elephantine in southern Egypt. These deal with a variety of topics, including marriage and divorce, and give us insight into the rather deviant Judaism practiced by the Jews who had settled there.[1]

However, there are other Jewish sources that are closer in time and space to the Gospels, and we will look at them in this chapter. First, from the second and first centuries BC we have the Dead Sea Scrolls. These texts are not only closest in time and space to the Gospels, but they also offer explicit commentary on the Old Testament teaching on divorce and critique their rivals' views with gusto. It is generally held that the Dead Sea Scrolls were written by a sect of Jews known elsewhere as the Essenes.[2] Their views were much stricter than mainstream Jews such as the Pharisees, whom they regarded as very lax "seekers after smooth things."

Second, from early Christian times, there is a mass of materials that are incorporated in the great collections of Jewish law

---

1. For details, see Bezalel Porten, "Elephantine Papyri," in David Noel Freedman, ed., *The Anchor Yale Bible Dictionary* (New York: Doubleday, 1992), 2:445–55.

2. John J. Collins, "Essenes," in *The Anchor Yale Bible Dictionary*, 2:619–26.

known as the Mishnah (AD 200) and Talmud (AD 500). The latter may be described as an expanded commentary on the Mishnah. These texts became normative in rabbinic Judaism, and their teaching on divorce has been central in discussions of the Gospel teaching.

THE DAMASCUS DOCUMENT AND THE TEMPLE SCROLL

We begin our review with two texts that probably originated in the second century BC: the Damascus Document and the Temple Scroll.[3] They were found among the Dead Sea Scrolls at Qumran, although the Damascus Document was already known from two medieval manuscripts found in a Cairo synagogue. These texts probably represent the views of an Essene group, the strictest party among the Jews in the first and second centuries BC. Essenes were most concerned about maintaining ritual purity in such areas as food and skin disease but also in sexual behavior, all issues that are discussed in the books of Leviticus and Deuteronomy (see especially Lev 11–18 and Deut 17–22). The Damascus Document and Temple Scroll are anxious to interpret the biblical texts in a conservative manner and to reject the more flexible interpretations of the Pharisees and Sadducees.

While they do not address the questions of divorce and remarriage explicitly, these texts give good insight into the fundamentals of Essene thinking about sex and marriage. For example, the incest regulations in Leviticus 18 and 20 are addressed to men and forbid males from marrying close female relatives. So, for example, a nephew may not marry his aunt (Lev 18:13), but nothing is said about the opposite case of an uncle marrying his niece.

---

3. Translations in Geza Vermes, *The Complete Dead Sea Scrolls in English* (London: Penguin Books, 2004), 127–47, 191–220.

How should this gap be interpreted? Does its silence about uncle-niece unions mean they are acceptable? (That was the view of mainstream Judaism.) Or should the rule be understood to apply reciprocally or inclusively? That is, if nephews may not marry aunts, then, by analogy, uncles may not marry nieces (the Essene view). In the Damascus Document, they accuse other Jews of flouting these laws:

> And each man marries the daughter of his brother or sister, whereas Moses said, *You shall not approach your mother's sister; she is your mother's near kin* (Lev 18:13). But although the laws against incest are written for men, they also apply to women. (Damascus Document, verses 8–11)[4]

This illustrates how these documents make the rules on marriage more restrictive than they were traditionally understood.

Even more illuminating is their handling of bigamy; they anticipate the Gospels in their appeal to Genesis for a much stricter stance on marrying more than once. Though the Old Testament recounts various episodes in the lives of the Patriarchs and other worthies that should discourage anyone from taking a second wife, polygamy is clearly not illegal. The king is expected to have more than one wife, as was the case with David and Solomon. The law in Deuteronomy 17:17 allows royal polygamy, merely insisting that the king should not have too many wives: "He shall not acquire many wives for himself lest his heart turn." In the scrolls, this law is said to apply not just to kings but to all who identify themselves as the true Israel, that is, the Essenes. In this way, their teaching is made stricter than that of mainstream Jews. Yet still greater strictness comes through their definition

---

4. Geza Vermes, *The Dead Sea Scrolls in English,* rev. and extended 4th ed. (Sheffield: Sheffield Academic Press, 1995), 100.

of "not many wives," which the Essenes understood to mean "just one wife." Their interpretation is supported by appeal to the opening chapters of Genesis. God created mankind in two sexes, male and female, thus implying that they should work together as couples, not in polygamous harems. The flood story tells how the animals entered the ark in pairs, understood by the Essenes as setting an example for humans to follow.

It is therefore clear that the author(s) of the scrolls rejected polygamy and insisted that the law required men to be monogamous. But how closely did they understand monogamy? It obviously rules out taking a second partner while the first is still alive. But what should be done when one party dies or the marriage is ended by divorce? Does the ban on second unions apply after one spouse has died or the marriage has ended in divorce? Interpreters disagree. The Temple Scroll does allow the king to remarry if he is widowed, but whether such liberty is allowed to ordinary lay folk is not so clear. Whichever interpretation is correct, it clearly implies a stricter approach to marriage than the mainstream Jewish view. In this respect, it could foreshadow the teaching of Jesus.

THE MISHNAH AND TALMUD

There is much more discussion of these issues in Jewish sources from the second century AD onward. The principal sources are the Mishnah and Talmud. The Mishnah is a collection of rabbinic sayings and rulings from the first two centuries that were brought together, organized, and written down about AD 200. The Talmud is a commentary on and expansion of the Mishnah that was committed to writing about AD 500. They both contain long sections devoted to expounding the rules and procedures in divorce as they developed in the first centuries of the Christian era.

Many of the sayings and legal decisions are ascribed to rabbis who lived and taught many years before the completion of the Mishnah and Talmud. Of particular relevance to our discussion are the sayings ascribed to rabbis Shammai and Hillel, who debated many issues in the last few years BC and in the opening years of the Christian era. Shammai represented the more conservative traditional school of thought in first-century Judaism, not as strict as the Essenes but more influential, whereas Hillel represented a more flexible approach to interpreting Old Testament law. The difference between them is immortalized in the story of a Gentile who told the rabbis that he would convert to Judaism if they could summarize for him everything it required of him while he stood on one foot. Shammai was so angered by the question that he drove the enquirer off with his stick. The Gentile then approached Hillel and asked the same question. He replied: "That which is despicable to you, do not do to your fellow, this is the whole Torah, and the rest is commentary, go and learn it."[5] It was eventually the school of Hillel that prevailed in mainstream rabbinic Judaism, but in the time of Christ the disputes between the schools of Shammai and Hillel were still unresolved and a matter of lively debate.

One of the areas of disagreement between these two schools of thought was divorce. Deuteronomy differentiates between divorce "because he has found some indecency in her" (24:1) and divorce for lesser causes, for instance the second husband "hates" her (24:3). The Hillelites, true to their easygoing approach to biblical law, said that a man could divorce his wife for any cause. For example, if she burned his supper or he saw a prettier woman,

---

5. Babylonian Talmud, *Shabbat* 31a.

the husband's right to divorce was absolute.[6] David Amram puts it this way: "This ancient right of the husband, to divorce his wife at his pleasure, is the central thought in the entire system of Jewish divorce law."[7] On the issue of divorce, it was the Hillelites who were upholding tradition, and the Shammaites who were challenging it. Like the Essenes, the Shammaites wanted a stricter sexual morality. They based their case on a phrase in Deuteronomy 24:1, "some indecency":[8]

> When a man takes a wife and marries her, if then she finds no favor in his eyes because he has found some indecency in her, and he writes her a certificate of divorce and puts it in her hand and sends her out of his house, and she departs out of his house, and if she goes and becomes another man's wife, and the latter man hates her and writes her a certificate of divorce.

The Shammaites argued that this law allows divorce only for "some indecency"—probably some sexual misbehavior serious enough to warrant her husband divorcing her and confiscating her dowry but not grave enough to warrant the death penalty, as adultery would be. To limit the husband's right to divorce whenever he chose and for any reason was for most Jews a shocking limitation on male freedom. It must have been highly controversial. Doubtless by asking Jesus' opinion, the Hillelites hoped to curb his popularity, as they guessed he would advocate a more restricted line than that favored by their own school.

6. Occasionally women initiated divorce, but the Talmud permits only men to sue for divorce.

7. David W. Amram, *The Jewish Law of Divorce according to Bible and Talmud with Some Reference to Its Development in Post-Talmudic Times* (1896; repr. New York: Hermon Press, 1975), 24.

8. Hebrew *erwath davar* literally means "nakedness of a thing"; see discussion in chapter 2 above.

This attempt to discredit him appears to be their motivation in the series of questions in Mark 11–12 about his authority, Roman taxes, the resurrection, and the great commandment. Mark says the questioners on these topics were sent "to trap him in his talk" (12:13). Similar motives may be surmised here. The more liberal Pharisees hoped that if Jesus came out in strong support of the conservative Shammaites, many Jews would be deterred from following him.

SUMMARY

While the Temple Scroll and Damascus Document found among the Dead Sea Scrolls do not explicitly speak about questions of divorce and remarriage, these texts give a good insight into Essene thinking about sex and marriage. They tended to make rules on marriage more restrictive than the more mainstream sects of Judaism in their day. In this respect, the teaching on marriage in the Dead Sea Scrolls could foreshadow the teaching of Jesus, but this is not certain.

From the Mishnah and Talmud, we learn more about the debates that were going on among rabbis closer to Jesus' day. The followers of Rabbi Hillel, in keeping with tradition, said that a man could divorce his wife for any cause. The followers of Rabbi Shammai argued that divorce was warranted for sexual misbehavior that was less serious than adultery, which could have required the death penalty. Therefore, when the Hillelites asked Jesus' opinion on the question of whether a man could divorce his wife for any reason, they probably thought he would side with the more restrictive Shammaites.

Having set the scene for the Gospel accounts of Jesus' dispute with the Pharisees, we must now examine the separate passages.

4.

—

MATTHEW 1
ON DIVORCE

There are four passages in the Gospels that explicitly discuss the legitimacy of divorce and remarriage: Matthew 5:31–32 (part of the Sermon on the Mount), Matthew 19:3–12 (Matthew's account of Jesus' clash with the Pharisees), Mark 10:2–12 (Mark's version of that episode), and Luke 16:18 (Luke's only reference to the issue). Conventional Gospel critics regard Luke 16:18 and Mark 10 as the earliest versions of the debate with the Pharisees and the Matthew texts as later versions of Jesus' teaching, but this is not universally agreed.[1]

Here I shall avoid the critical debates about dating the Gospels, usually referred to as the Synoptic problem, but instead look at the texts in their canonical order, Matthew > Mark > Luke. This is how Christians down the ages have read them and understood them. Furthermore, modern scholars now recognize the priority of reading the texts in their present final form before one engages in speculation about the date and development of these texts.

Before addressing those four passages, however, I would like to begin with a fifth text, Matthew 1:18–25. This does not explicitly discuss remarriage but does illustrate how adultery should be handled and shows how the exception clause in the other passages is supposed to function. So we begin our discussion by looking at Matthew's account of the annunciation to Joseph and his reaction. There are allusions to the Virgin Birth in John's Gospel (8:41), which reflect Jewish horror at extramarital affairs, but

---

1. See David R. Catchpole, "The Synoptic Divorce Material as a Traditio-Historical Problem," *Bulletin of the John Rylands Library* 57 (1974): 92–127.

they do not illuminate divorce practice, so I will limit our discussion to Matthew.

JOSEPH'S RIGHTEOUSNESS

Matthew's Gospel begins with a genealogy of Jesus the Christ the Son of David, which is appropriate in a Gospel designed to demonstrate that Jesus is the long-awaited king descended from David (Matt 1:1–17). This theme is very clear in chapter 2 with the visit of the wise men seeking the king of the Jews (Matt 2:1–12). In between, we have the account of the annunciation to Joseph. Its focus is on "Emmanuel—God with us," another important theme in this Gospel, reaching its conclusion with Jesus' words in Matthew 28:20, "I am with you always, to the end of the age."

The presence of these topics at the beginning of the biography of Jesus seems natural, but it is strange to have no account of his birth: it seems as though Matthew assumes his readers know Luke's infancy narrative either from oral tradition or written form.[2] But whatever the case, it is clear that he regards Joseph's reaction to Mary's pregnancy as more important than recording the details of Jesus' birth:

> Now the birth of Jesus Christ took place in this way. When his mother Mary had been betrothed to Joseph, before they came together she was found to be with child from the Holy Spirit. And her husband Joseph, being a just man and unwilling to put her to shame, resolved to divorce her quietly. But as he considered these things, behold, an angel of the Lord appeared to him in a dream, saying, "Joseph, son of David, do not fear to take Mary as your wife, for

---

2. So Luz: "It is as if the rule were that what Matthew reports does not appear in Luke and vice versa." Ulrich Luz, *Matthew 1–7: A Commentary,* rev. ed., Hermeneia (Minneapolis: Fortress Press, 2007), 75.

that which is conceived in her is from the Holy Spirit. She will bear a son, and you shall call his name Jesus, for he will save his people from their sins." ... When Joseph woke from sleep, he did as the angel of the Lord commanded him: he took his wife, but knew her not until she had given birth to a son. And he called his name Jesus. (Matt 1:18–21, 24–25)

Joseph's behavior gives an illuminating insight into how a righteous—that is, a Torah-keeping—man should treat his spouse if he suspects her of adultery. Under Old Testament and earlier Near Eastern law, a wife guilty of adultery could be executed as long as her lover was treated the same (see Deut 22:22 and the discussion in chapter 2). Proverbs pictures the offended husband refusing to waive his right to revenge (Prov 6:32–35). But there is no known case of the death penalty being applied, and it is generally held that divorce was the usual response to adultery. Indeed, the Mishnah insists that adulterous wives must be divorced.[3] This principle applies to betrothed women, for betrothal is more than a mere engagement to marry. It is inchoate marriage, whereby the bride passes from being subject to her father's authority to being under her future husband's authority (see above, pp. 10–11).

This was the situation in Mary's case: betrothed to Joseph, she was bound to be loyal to her future husband although they were not yet living together. That started after the wedding. Because they were inchoately married, Mary was seen as guilty of adultery and had to be divorced formally. This brought shame on both bride and groom and their families, and especially on the bride. Joseph, being a righteous man, wanted to avoid this: "her

---

3. Mishnah, *Ketubot* 3:4–5.

husband Joseph, being a just man and unwilling to put her to shame, resolved to divorce her quietly" (Matt 1:19).

It is not clear quite what Joseph does that demonstrates his righteousness. It could be his readiness to follow Jewish legal custom in divorcing his supposedly adulterous bride, or it could be his unwillingness to shame her publicly by bringing her to court. But maybe both motives were involved.[4] By characterizing Joseph's behavior as "just" or "righteous" (Greek *dikaios*), Matthew is affirming that it makes Joseph more than an example of a good Jew: he is a model for Christian action too.[5] This is confirmed by his obedience to the angelic instructions conveyed in dreams. It repeatedly says: "He did as the angel of the Lord commanded" or something equivalent (Matt 1:24; 2:14, 19, 21).[6]

THE ROYAL BIRTH AND JEWISH MARRIAGE CUSTOM

For our purposes, it is striking that the Gospel narrative should begin with a story about divorce. And it is not just some minor characters that are involved but the parents of the central figure in that story, Joseph and Mary. We have observed how the actions of Joseph are dictated by the conventions of Jewish law and marriage customs of the time. Mary is betrothed to Joseph and subject to his authority although she was not living with him.

---

4. Luz, *Matthew 1–7*, 95.

5. For righteousness as a mark of Christian discipleship, see Matt 5:6, 10; 25:37, 46.

6. Another example of Joseph's fidelity to Jewish custom may be alluded to in the final comment "but he knew her not until she had given birth to a son." Among Jews and other ancient peoples, sexual intercourse with one's pregnant wife was disapproved of. See Dale C. Allison, "Divorce, Celibacy and Joseph (Matthew 1:18–25 and 19:1–12)," *Journal for the Study of the New Testament* 49.1 (1993): 3–10; and Markus Bockmuehl, "Matthew 5:32, 19:9 in the Light of Pre-Rabbinic Halakhah," *New Testament Studies* 35.2 (1989): 291–95. The more obvious reason for mentioning Joseph's abstinence is to underline the divine origin of Jesus.

This is technically called inchoate marriage, and infidelity by the betrothed counts as adultery: this is why Joseph wanted to divorce her. Divorce was the usual penalty for sexual misbehavior. Though the Old Testament prescribes death for blatant adultery, under Near Eastern law the cuckolded husband did not have to enforce it if he was prepared to spare the guilty male. The lack of any record of the death penalty being enforced makes it probable that divorce, with all the financial costs discussed above, was the regular penalty. Of course, Joseph could not name the third party until the angel revealed it; that would have complicated divorce proceedings. However, as a righteous man, Joseph did not wish to make Mary a public disgrace, and so he decided to do it quietly. But why, if he wished to treat Mary gently, did he want to divorce her at all? Matthew does not explain: he assumes the reader will understand. Probably he felt obliged to divorce her because this was what first-century Jewish law and convention required. Husbands and fiancés (inchoate husbands) could not just overlook or forgive their unfaithful wives; they had to be divorced.

Coming right at the opening of Matthew's Gospel, this passage gives a glimpse of his presuppositions. We have already noted the royal Davidic messiah theme and the Son of God theme. But the passage also discloses some of the evangelist's assumptions about the law exemplified by Joseph's approach to marriage. The reactions of righteous Joseph show how others who would be righteous ought to behave. He finds himself obliged to divorce his bride because he believes her to be unfaithful, and this is how society requires a husband to treat his errant wife. That it is society that makes this demand is implied by his plan to put her away quietly. Craig S. Keener writes, "Under these circumstances, Joseph would be righteous in divorcing Mary; to fail to do so would violate law and custom, would bring enduring reproach on his household and would constitute embracing as wife one who had betrayed him in the worst manner conceivable in his culture."[7] Joseph recognized that it was his duty to divorce Mary if she was unfaithful, but he wanted to do it in a kindly way and not add to her shame.

Though one may read Matthew 1 as no more than an account of the circumstances of Jesus' birth, it is probably meant to be more than that. According to F. Dale Bruner, "The nativity is not often drawn into discussions of divorce in Matt 5 and 19. Our text seems to teach that a decision to divorce can in some cases be a form of *righteousness*, even in a Gospel that so counterculturally protects marriage against divorce."[8] Joseph's planned course of action shows how righteous husbands may divorce their wives if the law and society demand it. But there may be a hint about the undesirability of divorce, even if deserved, in the angel's intervention and in Joseph's unwillingness to make Mary a public example.

SUMMARY

The first mention of the birth of Jesus is written to explain his miraculous conception by the agency of the Holy Spirit. It thereby confirms and complements the birth narratives in Luke's Gospel. But incidentally this episode sheds light on first-century Jewish beliefs and marriage customs. It illustrates the significance of betrothal, in which the bride enters into inchoate marriage while not leaving her parental home: she passes from being subject to her father's authority to being under her fiancé's authority. This means that intercourse with a man who is not her future husband counts as adultery and requires him to divorce her.

---

7. Craig S. Keener, *Matthew*, The IVP New Testament Commentary Series (Downers Grove, IL: InterVarsity Press, 1997), 61.

8. F. Dale Bruner, *Matthew: A Commentary: The Christbook, Matthew 1–12*, rev. and expanded ed., vol. 1 (Grand Rapids: Eerdmans, 2007), 25.

This is what Joseph was going to do until the angel instructed him otherwise. He represents the reaction of a righteous Jew to this tricky situation, and his case needs to be borne in mind when we consider the texts explicitly discussing marriage and divorce. It seems that in cases of infidelity, divorce is not so much an option as the duty of the injured spouse.

5.

—

MATTHEW 5:31–32 ON DIVORCE

So far we have been looking at the background to Jesus' teaching on divorce in the Gospels. I have called on the marriage laws and customs of the ancient Near East and also Matthew's account of Jesus' birth to build a picture of the assumptions that Jesus, his disciples and opponents, and the evangelist Matthew would have had about marriage and divorce.

We now begin looking at the four passages that explicitly discuss divorce and remarriage in the Gospels, turning first to Jesus' remarks in the Sermon on the Mount.[1]

> It was also said, "Whoever divorces his wife, let him give her a certificate of divorce." But I say to you that everyone who divorces his wife, except on the ground of sexual immorality, makes her commit adultery, and whoever marries a divorced woman commits adultery. (Matt 5:31–32)

Here adultery is charged even without necessarily involving sexual intercourse: simply divorcing one's wife causes her to commit adultery, and marrying a divorced woman is also to commit adultery. The preface to these verses gives some helpful context:

> Do not think that I have come to abolish the Law or the Prophets; I have not come to abolish them but to fulfill

---

1. For helpful discussion of the main options see Ulrich Luz, *Matthew 1–7: A Commentary*, rev. ed., Hermeneia (Minneapolis: Fortress Press, 2007), 210–25; and J. P. Meier, *Law and History in Matthew's Gospel* (Rome: Biblical Institute Press, 1976).

them. For truly, I say to you, until heaven and earth pass away, not an iota, not a dot, will pass from the Law until all is accomplished. Therefore whoever relaxes one of the least of these commandments and teaches others to do the same will be called least in the kingdom of heaven, but whoever does them and teaches them will be called great in the kingdom of heaven. For I tell you, unless your righteousness exceeds that of the scribes and Pharisees, you will never enter the kingdom of heaven. (Matt 5:17–20)

Scholars debate what is meant by Jesus' fulfilling the law. In many ways, Matthew's usage makes clear that Jesus fulfills everything in the Old Testament: promises, law, history. But while the finer points are debated, it is clear that Jesus is putting forward a more demanding ethic than his hearers had known previously. Their righteousness must exceed that of the scribes and Pharisees. This is important to bear in mind when considering his teaching about marriage and divorce.

ANTITHESIS ABOUT ADULTERY

In Matthew 5, this teaching is part of the antithesis about adultery, which begins: "You have heard that it was said, 'You shall not commit adultery.' But I say to you …" (Matt 5:27–28). Here the prohibition of adultery is extended to include lust, thereby dramatically intensifying the old law's demands.

Everyone who looks at a woman with lustful intent has already committed adultery with her in his heart. If your right eye causes you to sin, tear it out and throw it away. For it is better that you lose one of your members than that your whole body be thrown into hell. And if your right hand causes you to sin, cut it off and throw it away. For it is better that you lose one of your members than that your whole body go into hell. (Matt 5:28–30)

The importance of this antithesis is underlined by the length of the expansion and its comprehensive coverage of different realms of action: thought = "lustful intent"; sight = "right eye"; touch = "right hand." And this is the only antithesis that contains the repeated warning that failure to heed it could lead to your whole body being thrown into hell.

These new definitions of adultery that do not necessarily involve sexual intercourse show they are not to be taken literally; but by calling divorce by itself adultery, and lust, etc., adultery, Jesus is saying such behavior is as serious as adultery. This is reinforced with the added threat of hell, which is both shocking and frightening, but it must inform our understanding of Jesus' teaching that divorce may count as adultery. If adultery can have such dire eternal consequences, it must at all costs be avoided.

JESUS' COMMENT ON DEUTERONOMY 24

After two antitheses explicitly based on the Decalogue (anger in Matt 5:21–26 and lust in verses 27–30) comes another that further redefines the scope of an Old Testament law. In chapter 2, we looked at Deuteronomy 24:1–4 for the light it sheds on Old Testament divorce practice. We now return to it to see Jesus' comment on it.

Deuteronomy 24:1–4 deals with the case of a divorced man who wants to remarry his first wife, her second husband having died or been divorced. Deuteronomy 24:4 forbids this. Why remarriage was forbidden has been much discussed, and I have given what I think is the most likely explanation on pages 26–30 above.

> When a man takes a wife and marries her, if then she finds
> no favor in his eyes because he has found some indecency
> in her, and he writes her a certificate of divorce and puts it
> in her hand and sends her out of his house, and she departs
> out of his house, and if she goes and becomes another
> man's wife, and the latter man hates her and writes her
> a certificate of divorce and puts it in her hand and sends
> her out of his house, or if the latter man dies, who took
> her to be his wife, then her former husband, who sent her
> away, may not take her again to be his wife. (Deut 24:1–4)

It is not necessary to review the Old Testament setting of
this law or its reasoning here because the debate between Jesus
and the Pharisees does not turn on this. Rather, it turns only
on the certificate of divorce and the phrase "ground of sexual
immorality."

> It was also said, "Whoever divorces his wife, let him give
> her a certificate of divorce." But I say to you that every-
> one who divorces his wife, except on the ground of sexual
> immorality, makes her commit adultery, and whoever
> marries a divorced woman commits adultery. (Matt
> 5:31–32)

Deuteronomy 24 just mentions the giving of a divorce certificate as part of the regular procedure for divorce. In Deuteronomy,
this is not a command, whereas it is in the loose paraphrase of
Matthew 5:31. This is how the Pharisees read it and used it to
justify divorce.

But Jesus, having enlarged the scope of adultery to cover lustful looks in verse 28, now broadens it further to cover divorce,
which is an awesome condemnation in the context of verses
29–30 with their threats of hell for transgressors. Verses 31–32

speak only of the husband divorcing his wife. This fits the situation in a culture where only males initiated divorce. It would certainly not be viewed as adultery by first-century Jews. As Amram puts it: "This ancient right of the husband, to divorce his wife at his pleasure, is the central thought in the entire system of Jewish divorce law; and the Rabbis did not, nor could they, set it aside, although ... they gradually tempered its severity by numerous restrictive measures."[2]

A NEW DEFINITION OF ADULTERY

As we saw in the previous chapter, Joseph's readiness to divorce Mary is an example of this right being presupposed by Joseph and his family. She, they supposed, had been unfaithful and therefore by Jewish law had to be divorced.[3] Indeed, it was because Joseph was a just (righteous) man that he intended to do it (Matt 1:19). Thus in allowing divorce for "sexual immorality" (Greek *porneia*) to escape censure, Jesus is not breaking with Jewish tradition. It is in his expanding the notion of adultery to cover divorce for other reasons that Jesus is being original and radical. His new definition of adultery that included divorce in all situations except where the wife was guilty of immorality was a huge innovation. This ruling threw out the husband's age-old right to divorce his wife for any cause. It also introduced the idea that husbands could be guilty of committing adultery against their own wives; until then adultery was just seen as an offense against the husband, never against the wife.

The last saying in Matthew 5:32, "whoever marries a divorced woman commits adultery," enlarges the definition of adultery yet further. The vital element in a divorce certificate is the

---

2. David W. Amram, *The Jewish Law of Divorce according to Bible and Talmud with Some Reference to Its Development in Post-Talmudic Times* (1896; repr. New York: Hermon Press, 1975), 24

3. Amram, *Jewish Law of Divorce*, 35.

declaration "You are free to marry any man," because a primary function of divorce is to protect the divorced woman from the accusation of adultery should she marry again. By saying that marriage to a divorcee is adultery, Jesus is declaring that the divorce proceedings and the divorce certificate do not achieve what they purport to do: that is, freeing the woman to marry again.

For Jesus, the divorced wife is not free to marry any man. Indeed, no one can marry her without committing adultery. The implication of this redefinition of adultery is that the marriage has not been dissolved by divorce. This may sound like a restriction on the woman's rights, but in fact it puts husband and wife on an equal footing for the first time: both are bound to be completely loyal to each other, whereas under the Old Testament and later Jewish law a double standard operated. This required wives to be totally loyal to their husbands and suffer as adulteresses if they were not faithful. But husbands were not so restricted. If they had affairs, that was not regarded as adultery. This is not to say affairs by husbands were approved; they were tolerated and the couple involved did not risk the death penalty. If husbands were not required to have only one sexual partner, it followed that taking a second wife or even several wives was legal. So while the Old Testament sees monogamy as the divine ideal, it does not rule out bigamy and polygamy.[4] This continued to be the Jewish position until the eleventh century AD, when polygamy was banned by the decree of Rabbi Gershom (c. AD 1025).[5] This was a major innovation because the rabbis did not ordinarily permit their rulings to ban what was permitted in the Old Testament, and polygamy, though not common in Old Testament times, was certainly

4. Gordon J. Wenham, *Story as Torah: Reading the Old Testament Ethically* (Edinburgh: T&T Clark, 2000), 85–86.

5. Amram, *Jewish Law of Divorce*, 52–53.

allowed and practiced by some very respectable people, such as kings and Patriarchs.[6]

This hasty review of the Sermon on the Mount's teaching on divorce and adultery is a good example of how Jesus *by* endorsing a husband's right to divorce an unfaithful wife reasserted the validity of the Old Testament law: "Do not think I have come to abolish the Law and the Prophets." At the same time, he made it more restrictive. One might say that he extended its scope and insisted that people's righteousness must exceed that of the scribes and Pharisees when he declared that all divorces, except those for immorality, were adulterous. He thus both declared the law's eternal relevance (Matt 5:18) and explained how it should be applied more strictly. Dupont sums up the implications as follows:

> Jesus does not say in a general abstract sort of way: "divorce does not dissolve the marriage." He describes a concrete situation, that of a divorced woman, and declares to him who wants to marry her that this marriage is adultery. This woman whom a divorce has liberated is not free. Contradictory? Not at all, but a way of making us feel more vividly a quite new teaching, which deprives divorce of its essence. Jesus keeps the term, but changes its content. This freed woman is not really free: the dissolved marriage still exists. In speaking as he does, Jesus makes his hearers realise that divorce has no effect on the marriage bond: although separated, the spouses remain united by the marriage. That is why a new marriage would be adultery.[7]

---

6. Amram, *Jewish Law of Divorce,* 53.

7. J. Dupont, *Mariage et divorce dans l'évangile* (Bruges: Desclée de Brouwer, 1959), 57.

SUMMARY

Let us sum up the changes to earlier Old Testament and Jewish law that Jesus is advocating in the Sermon.

1. Adultery includes lustful thoughts ("adultery in the heart").

2. Adultery may involve the senses of sight and touch (eye, hand).

3. Divorce, by being put on a par with adultery, is as serious as adultery.

4. Adultery is involved in the remarriage of divorcees.

5. Divorce does not terminate a marriage.

6. Bigamy and polygamy are kinds of adultery.

7. God may punish adulterers by consigning them to hell.

These extensions of the definition of adultery amount to saying that divorce with the right to marry any man is impossible. Married persons may separate but not divorce and remarry.

Some of these deeds and attitudes were disapproved of by the Essenes and later rabbis, but the fierce condemnation by Jesus is revolutionary. Particularly striking is his description of marriage after divorce as adultery. This implies that the marriage bond is eternal and that any second union such as bigamy is prohibited. In so doing, he abolished the double standard and gave women true equality with men. Under the old regime, a wife had to be exclusively loyal to her husband, but he did not have the same obligation to be totally loyal to her. If he had an affair or took a second wife, this did not count as committing adultery against her. But by declaring that remarriage constituted adultery, Jesus curbed the husband's traditional freedom. Thus he introduced full monogamy and true reciprocity between the sexes as regards conjugal rights and duties.

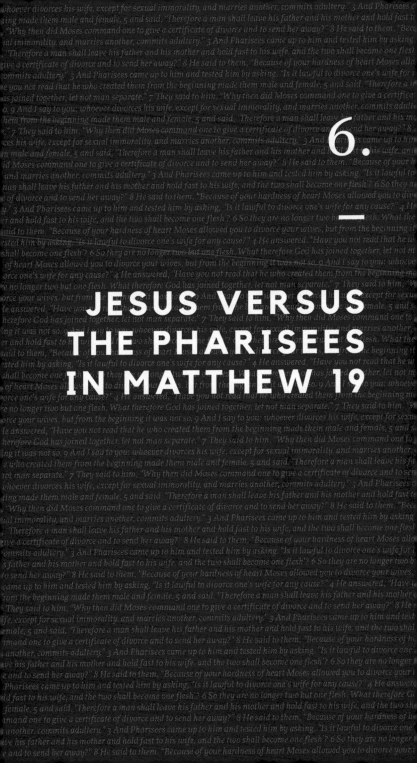

6.

JESUS VERSUS THE PHARISEES IN MATTHEW 19

Jesus' remarks in the Sermon on the Mount challenged many accepted principles on various issues including those to do with marriage and divorce. As we have seen, a Jewish man could divorce his wife for any reason, though it might be costly if divorce meant he lost control of his wife's dowry. Jesus says divorce for any reason, unless prompted by the wife's immorality, constitutes adultery. In other words, divorce is forbidden in most cases. This has further ramifications: Most first-century Jews thought a man could have more than one wife, or if he had an affair, he was not guilty of adultery against his wife. They accepted the double standard which demanded total loyalty from wives but not from husbands. Jesus, on the other hand, ruled out the double standard and banned polygamy, or bigamy, as well as male infidelity. His warnings about the danger of being tempted to sin by one's eye or one's hand could be seen as criticizing the common tendency to blame the female for tempting men to sin. In short, it could be described as an outright attack on the chauvinism of the rabbis.

Therefore, it is no surprise that the scribes and Pharisees, who saw themselves as upholding orthodoxy, reacted strongly. Matthew 19:3–12 (parallel Mark 10:2–12) recounts their attempt to refute Jesus' teaching:

And Pharisees came up to him and tested him by asking, "Is it lawful to divorce one's wife for any cause?" He answered, "Have you not read that he who created them from the beginning made them male and female and said, "Therefore a man shall leave his father and his mother and hold fast to his wife, and the two shall become one flesh"?

So they are no longer two but one flesh. What therefore God has joined together, let not man separate." They said to him, "Why then did Moses command one to give a certificate of divorce and to send her away?" He said to them, "Because of your hardness of heart Moses allowed you to divorce your wives, but from the beginning it was not so. And I say to you: whoever divorces his wife, except for sexual immorality, and marries another, commits adultery." (Matt 19:3–9)

The Pharisees are said to have come to test Jesus by asking: "Is it lawful to divorce one's wife for any cause?" This term "test" comes several times in the last days of Jesus' ministry in Jerusalem (Matt 16:1; 22:18, 35). Testing in this context does not mean an open-minded evaluation of his teaching but attempting to catch Jesus out and get him to say something that would incriminate him in the eyes of the authorities and dampen his popularity with ordinary people. If Jesus ruled out the right to divorce "for any cause," this would, they hoped, achieve both aims very well. He would be considered as extreme as the Shammaites and Essenes, who both limited the right to divorce but did not abolish it. Similar motives are very clear when he was asked about the legitimacy of paying taxes to Caesar (Matt 22:15–22; compare 22:34–46). They hoped his response would damn him in the eyes of the Sanhedrin and destroy his reputation as a prophet among those who came to listen to his preaching.

But, as on other occasions of testing, Jesus turned the tables on his questioners. Undeterred by the possibility of unpopularity, he went further than any other group in Judaism of the time in outlawing traditional divorce completely. He permitted divorce where the wife had misbehaved sexually, but unlike other teachers he denied these divorcees the right to remarry. He based his stand on the creation story, quoting Genesis 1:27 ("male and female he created them") and 2:24 ("Therefore a man shall leave his father and his mother and hold fast to his wife, and the two shall become one flesh").

The Pharisees had invited Jesus to comment on the debate between the great rabbis Hillel and Shammai and say whose side he was on. But Jesus denies that this was a topic for academic debate, for the Creator himself had created man in two sexes so that when they meet, they become one flesh, that is, as closely related to each other as brother and sister or parent and child. These are relationships that cannot be undone. "What therefore God has joined together, let not man separate." By this appeal to Genesis, Jesus transposed the debate to a different key. Divorce was not possible under certain circumstances defined by some rabbi; it was impossible because it clashed with the Creator's intentions in creating marriage. Genesis makes traditional divorce impossible. The divorced couple, though separated from each other, are still related to each other in the one-flesh union. This means that any third-party relationship on the part of either the ex-husband or the ex-wife is adultery.

The Pharisees do not dispute Jesus' logic. Instead, they appeal to the greatest of the rabbis, Moses, the mediator of the law, which they held was the very Word of God. They quoted Deuteronomy 24, "Why then did Moses command one to give a certificate of divorce and to send her away?" (Matt 19:7).

It is not quite accurate to say Moses *commanded* divorce in Deuteronomy: the divorce procedure is mentioned just as the background to the prohibition on remarriage in Deuteronomy 24:3.[1] Jesus is not fazed by their appeal to the law. He argues that the need for a law on divorce proved their sinfulness, not their

---

1. See discussion above, p. 27.

piety. "He said to them, 'Because of your hardness of heart Moses allowed you to divorce your wives.'" Divorce is contrary to the Creator's design, but "from the beginning it was not so."

This clinches the argument, but Jesus does not leave it there. He draws out the practical implications for "from the beginning it was not so." He ends by reaffirming the point he made at the outset in the Sermon on the Mount (Matt 5:32; compare 19:9): "whoever divorces his wife, except for sexual immorality, and marries another, commits adultery." As we saw above, this prohibits any second marriage and allows divorce without remarriage only when the wife is guilty of sexual immorality. This is stricter than the school of Shammai, who allowed divorce in cases of immorality with the right to marry again. And of course it was much stricter than the Hillelites, who permitted divorce and remarriage for any cause. Thus Matthew portrays Jesus giving a clear and emphatic answer to the Pharisees' question: "Is it lawful to divorce one's wife for any cause?"

This hard ruling prompts the disciples to protest: "If such is the case of a man with his wife, it is better not to marry" (Matt 19:10). In other words, it is better to be single than irrevocably tied to a difficult spouse. Often the connection between the divorce debate (verses 3–9) and the eunuch sayings (verses 10–12) is overlooked. Excluding remarriage prompts Jesus to talk about eunuchs, that is, men who are unable to enjoy a full married life. It is better, with several modern writers,[2] to see them as seamlessly linked.

---

2. For example, Dupont, *Mariage et divorce*; Quentin Quesnell, "Made Themselves Eunuchs for the Kingdom of Heaven (Mt 19,12)," *Catholic Biblical Quarterly* 30 (1968): 335–58; William A. Heth and Gordon J. Wenham, *Jesus and Divorce* (London: Hodder & Stoughton, 1984); Ulrich Luz, *Matthew 1–7: A Commentary*, rev. ed., Hermeneia (Minneapolis: Fortress Press, 2007), 496–503.

One rarely noticed mark of the unity of Matthew 19:3–12 is to see them as following the pattern of a challenge to a teacher. Just a few verses after the divorce debate comes the story of the rich young man who came to ask Jesus what he had to do to gain eternal life (Matt 19:16–30). Both passages proceed in a similar order. The following table sets the two episodes in parallel columns.

	Rich Young Man Matthew 19:16–30	Divorce Debate Matthew 19:3–12
Someone asks a question	What good deed must I do? (16)	Is it lawful? (3)
Jesus challenges basis of question	Why do you ask me? (17)	Have you not read? (4–6)
Opponents counterattack, raising objections from Scripture	Which ones? (18–20)	Why did Moses? (7)
Jesus dismisses objections	Go sell what you possess (21–24)	Because of your hardness (8–9)
Disciples express their difficulties with the teaching	Who then can be saved? (25)	If such is the case ... better not to marry (10)
Jesus reaffirms his teaching and challenges hearers to have faith and accept it	With man this is impossible ... with God all things are possible (26)	Let the one who is able to receive this receive it (11–12)

Mark's version of the Rich Young Man account is structured similarly to Matthew's. To suppose that the divorce debate ends at Matthew 19:9 is to truncate an integral unit: verses 10–12 make an appropriate conclusion to the debate. They are not ill-considered add-ons.

The content also builds progressively to a climax. This pattern highlights a very important point: Jesus does not back down or make concessions to the original questioner or to the disciples when they object to his teaching. For example, the Pharisees say: "Why then did Moses command one to give a certificate of divorce?" Jesus counterattacks: "Because of your hardness of heart Moses allowed you to divorce your wives, but from the beginning it was not so." We should now expect Jesus to reject the Pharisees' views explicitly. And this is what he does: "whoever divorces his wife, except for sexual immorality, and marries another, commits adultery" rules out both the Hillelite divorce for any cause and the Shammaite divorce and remarriage only for sexual immorality, for Jesus—while allowing separation for immorality—does not permit remarriage. By permitting divorce (that is, separation) only for sexual immorality, and by ruling out remarriage, Jesus shows that his views are quite different from both Pharisaic positions. Both Hillelites and Shammaites allowed remarriage after divorce; they differed only over what grounds warranted divorce.

If remarriage even for the innocent party was ruled out, it is little wonder that the disciples were shocked and protested sharply: "If such is the case of a man with his wife, it is better not to marry." This is a total denial of all Jesus' teaching up to this point, for the whole thrust of the passage has been toward the building up of the greatness and sanctity before God of monogamous marriage.[3]

Jesus' response should not be read as conceding the disciples' point, as it would be if verses 11–12 were understood simply as a call to celibacy. This would be incongruous after the appeal to Genesis to prove marriage was part of the divine plan to create mankind in two sexes to be fruitful and multiply. Nor is it adequate to see verses 1–9 and 10–12 as originally independent sayings whose meaning is unchanged when linked together as in the present text. Furthermore, such a reading misses the usual role of speeches by disciples in controversy stories. "The ordinary function of the disciples' speeches is to ask questions, to misunderstand or to object, or simply to advance the action dramatically. They do not enunciate the Christian ideal for life. The objections are not accepted or confirmed by the Master, but are refuted or made the occasion for stronger restatement of the original teaching."[4]

Verses 10–12 do just this if they are understood to describe the plight of a married man whose wife has committed adultery or some other serious fault. In consequence, both of them are divorced. He is left on his own and unable to remarry. This makes him like a eunuch who cannot marry. Some eunuchs are born that way, others are made eunuchs by men, and yet others have made themselves eunuchs for the sake of the kingdom of heaven. This third group comprises those who are voluntarily single out of obedience to Christ's teaching. In the present context, it must primarily refer to stranded divorcees, but in other contexts, it could refer to those who adopt a single life voluntarily to serve Christ with undivided loyalty; prominent examples include Paul

---

3. Quesnell, "Made Themselves Eunuchs," 342.

4. Quesnell, "Made Themselves Eunuchs," 343.

and Jesus himself. Read this way, Matthew 19:3–12 is coherent and logical, building to a climax in the fashion typical of Jesus' disputes with his opponents.[5]

POSTSCRIPT: SOME ALTERNATIVE INTERPRETATIONS

It was not my purpose in writing this work to give yet another review of the scholarly debates about the interpretation of the Gospel divorce sayings. That may be found in *Jesus and Divorce,* among other places,[6] but as there has been some movement in scholarly opinion in the last thirty or so years, we need to give a brief review of the main points of contention. These center on Matthew 19, as it is the only passage which is open to the possibility that a divorcee is allowed to remarry. So far, we have looked only at the most probable interpretation, which excludes such a possibility.

But there are other interpretations, and these hinge on two main issues: the first is the meaning of the Greek term *porneia,* translated in the ESV, NIV, and NKJV as "sexual immorality."[7] If *porneia* could be more narrowly defined, the clash between Jesus' original teaching, which did not permit remarriage, and Matthew's revised understanding, which it is alleged did allow it, could be eliminated.

The other issue involves the grammar of the exception clause "except for sexual immorality." Does the exception cover both verbs in the main clause, "divorce" and "marry"? Or does it apply only to the first verb, "divorce"? In the first case, we could expand the whole saying to: "whoever divorces his wife, and marries

---

5. Compare Quesnell, "Made Themselves Eunuchs," 346–47.

6. Luz, *Matthew 1–7,* 488–96.

7. Compare other translations: KJV "fornication"; RSV, NRSV "unchastity."

another, commits adultery," and: "whoever divorces his wife for sexual immorality, and marries another, does not commit adultery." In the second case, we could expand the saying to: "whoever divorces his wife, and marries another, commits adultery," and: "whoever divorces his wife for sexual immorality, and marries another, commits adultery." The present text of Matthew 19:9 could be described as an elliptical summary of the two cases. We must now explain these options in more detail and evaluate them briefly.

THE MEANING OF *PORNEIA* AND THE EXCEPTION CLAUSE

The first issue to consider is the dictionary meaning of the key term *porneia*. The standard New Testament Greek dictionary defines *porneia* as "unlawful sexual intercourse, *prostitution, unchastity, fornication*."[8] It therefore covers all kinds of sexual sin, including incest, homosexuality, premarital intercourse, and adultery, doubtless the commonest fault. The term is a broad umbrella, one whose sense in a particular passage is determined by the context. In Matthew 19, it translates the Hebrew term *erwath davar*, literally "the nakedness of a thing." This is the term used in Deuteronomy 24:1 and translated "some indecency" in the ESV. The context does not help much to explain the exact sense of the Hebrew term. But if the surmise is correct that it refers to some behavior by the wife sufficiently serious that she forfeited her dowry when she was divorced (see above, p. 28), it would fit well with the dictionary definition. However, the translation "sexual immorality" does not sit well with the common interpretation, which allows remarriage as well as

---

8. William Arndt et al., *A Greek-English Lexicon of the New Testament and Other Early Christian Literature* (Chicago: University of Chicago Press, 2000), 854, italics original.

divorce for any cause, for this makes Jesus only agree with the stricter Shammaite Pharisees instead of reaffirming God's intention that marriage should be permanent. In fact, he once again expands the scope of the law instead of limiting it.

We have seen how in the debate with the Pharisees Jesus rebuts the views of both the liberal Hillelites and then the more conservative Shammaites, and finally concludes by answering the doubts of the disciples. At no point does he concede that they may have a point. Marriage is permanent, full stop, so Jesus challenges all who want to follow him to embrace the principle of no remarriage after divorce: "Let the one who is able to receive this receive it" (Matt 19:12).

Though the no-remarriage view makes excellent sense of the debate with the Pharisees, it has until recently been rejected or ignored by the majority of Protestant exegetes. This requires explanation. None of the other Gospels or Paul so much as hint that Jesus allowed remarriage after divorce. Then why have many New Testament scholars not taken the no-remarriage interpretation seriously? I fear that there may be an element of anti-Catholic prejudice involved, but another very significant factor is the accepted theories about the composition of the Gospels and the way Jesus' sayings have been preserved. Since Matthew drew on earlier sources, it is concluded that Jesus taught there should be no divorce or remarriage. This policy was then found to be too hard in practice, so it is surmised that Matthew's church adopted a more flexible regime, which allowed those divorced for their spouse's infidelity to marry again.

This view of the development of the Gospel traditions, that their particular features represent the ideas current in different churches, has been widely accepted. But this model of Gospel development has been fundamentally questioned by Richard Bauckham, who points to various hints that the Gospels are based on eyewitness testimony.[9] I am not building my case on this understanding of the growth of the Gospels, merely citing it to show the uncertainty of their composition and therefore the folly of resting a case on unproven critical theories. What is required is a coherent reading of the present text, not an interpretation based on a hypothetical reconstruction of some earlier text. As we have seen, the common critical approach makes the present version self-contradictory and makes the author of Matthew's Gospel a ham-fisted editor.[10] Readings that respect his literary skill and allow the account of the debate to unfold smoothly are much to be preferred.

In *Jesus and Divorce,* William Heth and I expounded and then critiqued six alternatives to the no-remarriage view. Here I give just brief summaries of three of the most popular alternative views. Their common aim is to eliminate, or at least minimize, the conflict between Jesus' no-remarriage position and the supposedly limited-remarriage view of the present Gospel text. Basically, if *porneia* can be defined very narrowly, the tension between Jesus' no-remarriage view and Matthew's Gospel, which supposedly allows remarriage for *porneia,* can be minimized.

1. One proposal is to take *porneia* to mean "incest" and see it as referring to the sort of unions listed

---

9. Richard Bauckham, *Jesus and the Eyewitnesses: the Gospels as Eyewitness Testimony,* 2nd ed. (Grand Rapids: Eerdmans, 2017), 114–47.

10. Catchpole elaborates, first, that "verses 10–12 do not arise out of verses 3–9" because he thinks celibacy is inconsistent with Jesus' praise of marriage in verses 4–8. Second, "verse 9 does not cohere with verses 4–8," because these verses rule out divorce absolutely, whereas verse 9 permits divorce in some cases. Third, "verses 4–8 do not cohere with verse 3b." In 3b the Pharisees ask about grounds for divorce, but Jesus' reply does not address that question. Fourth, "Verse 3b does not cohere with verse 3a." Catchpole describes 3a as a catch question designed to trap Jesus, whereas 3b is a straightforward question about the law. See David R. Catchpole, "The Synoptic Divorce Material as a Traditio-Historical Problem," *Bulletin of the John Rylands Library* 57 (1974): 99.

in Leviticus 18 and 20. For example, "you shall not uncover the nakedness of your sister" (Lev 18:9). Clearly, an incestuous marriage can and should be dissolved. There is some evidence that Gentile converts were unaware of the Old Testament incest rules, and that is why the Jerusalem council addressed the issue (Acts 15:20).

But while incestuous relationships could be described as *porneia,* they acquire this sense only from the context. Thus to limit the Jerusalem council's condemnation of *porneia* to incest may be to narrow *porneia* too tightly. As leader of the Jerusalem church, James would have shared the conviction of Jewish Christians that all kinds of sexual immorality were to be rejected. There are other sexual sins mentioned in Leviticus 18–20 to which James may also be alluding. *Porneia* is an umbrella term that can apply to many unlawful sexual actions.[11]

2. Similar to the incest view is the betrothal view, which would allow a fiancé to dissolve an engagement to his unfaithful fiancée and marry someone else. It also eliminates the contradiction between Jesus' no-remarriage position and the allegedly limited-remarriage view of the present Gospel text by supposing that *porneia* has the narrow sense of a bride having intercourse with a man who was not her fiancé. This was seen as adultery in Old

---

11. For further discussion, see Heth and Wenham, *Jesus and Divorce,* 151–68.

Testament and Jewish law and was the offense Joseph suspected in Mary (see above, p. 52).

Porneia would certainly include the sin of premarital, as well as postmarital, adultery and other sexual sins, but unless the wider context requires it, there is no reason to restrict its sense to premarital adultery; as already mentioned, *porneia* is an umbrella term.[12]

3. A third way of minimizing the conflict between Jesus' absolute rejection of divorce and the present Gospel text is to take the exceptive clause as an aside. This is the so-called preteritive view, where Matthew 19:9 could be paraphrased: "If anyone dismisses his wife—*porneia* is not involved—and marries another, he commits adultery."

    This is a neat solution to the problem, but it is difficult to justify grammatically. The so-called exceptive clause (*mē epi porneia*) is not being understood as a clause but as a parenthetical phrase, and it is unlikely that it can be construed that way. It must be taken as an elliptical conditional clause. The only way to understand *mē epi porneia* (not for sexual immorality) is as an ellipsis for a longer conditional clause "if he does not put her away for sexual immorality." The full statement then becomes "whoever puts away his wife, if he does not put her away for sexual immorality, and marries another, commits adultery."[13]

---

12. For further discussion, see Heth and Wenham, *Jesus and Divorce*, 169–78.

13. Dupont, *Mariage et divorce,* cited in Heth and Wenham, *Jesus and Divorce*, 188.

The difficulties with these three approaches to explaining the sense of the exceptive clause have led to them being abandoned by more recent writers who tend to revert to accepting the contrast between Jesus' words and the present Gospel text despite its incoherence when read this way. This incoherence is explained diachronically, that is, by the way the words of Jesus were modified by one or more editors as was needed in the different churches in which the Gospel was read. However, it is not explained why the final author or editor of the Gospel was unconcerned by the inconsistencies in the final text.

But the recent three-volume commentary on Matthew by Ulrich Luz is different. While indulging in a certain amount of tradition criticism, Luz comes down firmly on reading the final text as endorsing a no-remarriage view: "For Jesus divorce is absolutely forbidden except in the case of *porneia*—a term which refers to every form of inappropriate sexual activity on the wife's part, especially adultery."[14]

But does the exception clause apply only to the first verb in the clause, "divorces," or to both verbs "divorces" and "marries"? Luz thinks Matthew 19:9 should be read in the light of 5:32: "But I say to you that everyone who divorces his wife, except on the ground of sexual immorality, makes her commit adultery, and whoever marries a divorced woman commits adultery." Thus, "the prohibition of remarriage for a divorced man in 19:9 corresponds to the prohibition in 5:32 against remarrying a divorced woman."[15]

---

14. Luz, *Matthew 8–20: A Commentary,* Hermeneia (Minneapolis: Fortress Press, 2001), 492.

15. Luz, *Matthew 8–20,* 493. For an alternative way of relating 5:32 and 19:9, see Gordon J. Wenham, "The Syntax of Matthew 19:9," *Journal for the Study of the New Testament* 28 (1986): 17–23; and Wenham, "Matthew and Divorce: An Old Crux Revisited," *Journal for the Study of the New Testament* 22 (1984): 95–107.

Finally, he observes that the no-remarriage view "makes the negative reaction of the disciples in v. 10 more understandable."[16]

SUMMARY

Matthew 19:3–12 offers the fullest treatment of Jesus' teaching on marriage and divorce, and for that very reason has proved most contentious among Bible scholars. Often the evangelist is accused of muddle and self-contradiction. But I argue that it is unnecessary to belittle Matthew's writing skill in this way if he is endorsing a no-remarriage view.

The debate with the Pharisees brings out the distinctiveness of Jesus' teaching. Challenged by the Pharisees, Jesus reaffirmed his revolutionary position on marriage. Divorce followed by remarriage is tantamount to adultery. This implies that divorce does not terminate a marriage. It further implies that bigamy, polygamy, and the double standard which allowed more license to men than to women are wrong. Asked to arbitrate between the liberal Hillelite Pharisees, who permitted divorce and remarriage for any cause, and the conservative Shammaites, who allowed divorce and remarriage only for sexual immorality, Jesus denounced both views. In cases of immorality he allowed only separation, that is, divorce without the right to remarry.[17] He based his case on the Word of the Creator, whose authority was incomparably greater than any rabbi, whether Hillel, Shammai, or Moses. The debate closed with Jesus challenging innocent divorcees to follow in his footsteps as eunuchs for the kingdom of heaven.

---

16. Luz, *Matthew 8–20,* 493.

17. As mentioned above, it may well be that the evangelist Matthew approved the divorce of adulterers.

7.

DIVORCE IN THE OTHER GOSPELS

The other Gospels have less to say about divorce than Matthew. John includes nothing specific about divorce, Luke only one verse, and Mark eleven. We begin with the latter.

MARK 10:2–12

> And Pharisees came up and in order to test him asked, "Is it lawful for a man to divorce his wife?" He answered them, "What did Moses command you?" They said, "Moses allowed a man to write a certificate of divorce and to send her away." And Jesus said to them, "Because of your hardness of heart he wrote you this commandment. But from the beginning of creation, 'God made them male and female.' 'Therefore a man shall leave his father and mother and hold fast to his wife, and the two shall become one flesh.' So they are no longer two but one flesh. What therefore God has joined together, let not man separate."
>
> And in the house the disciples asked him again about this matter. And he said to them, "Whoever divorces his wife and marries another commits adultery against her, and if she divorces her husband and marries another, she commits adultery." (Mark 10:2–12)

Verses 2–9 are substantially the same as the parallel in Matthew 19:3–9. However, a number of minor differences may support the suggestion that while Matthew is written for Christians with a Jewish background, Mark's Gospel is written for Gentile believers, or at least for people unfamiliar with Jewish law. For example, in Mark the Pharisees ask: "Is it lawful for a man to divorce his wife?" which is a straightforward question about the principle of divorce. In Matthew, however, they ask for Jesus' opinion on a much debated issue among first-century Jewish rabbis: "Is it lawful to divorce one's wife for any cause?" This last phrase, "for any cause," shows they wanted him to pronounce on the dispute between the Hillelites, who allowed divorce for any cause, and the Shammaites, who did not. Another simplification of the debate is the omission of the exception clause. As both Jewish and Roman law required adulteresses to be divorced, there was no real difference from Matthew, since Mark brands remarriage as adultery. Thus the implications of Mark's presentation of the debate are much the same as Matthew's. There are other minor differences in the way the teaching of Jesus is introduced in verses 3–4, but they do not alter the practical outcome.

It is in the coda to the debate that the most significant differences between the two versions are to be seen. Matthew 19:10–12 deals with the consequences of a no-remarriage policy, particularly the plight of the innocent stranded husband who is likened to a eunuch. Mark 10:10–12 does not address this issue at all but focuses on how a no-remarriage policy affects women.

Under traditional Jewish law a wife could not initiate divorce. "The woman was never entitled to divorce her husband in Jewish law. Such an act would have been in opposition to the fundamental theory that divorce was the exclusive right of the husband."[1] This would seem to make it superfluous for Jesus to say: "if she divorces her husband and marries another, she commits adultery." But under Roman law, wives could sue for divorce, and this saying probably reflects this situation at least in the Herodian household,

---

1. David W. Amram, *The Jewish Law of Divorce according to Bible and Talmud with Some Reference to Its Development in Post-Talmudic Times* (1896; repr. New York: Hermon Press, 1975), 60.

where Herod the Great's sister Salome and his grand-daughter Herodias sent their husbands divorce certificates.[2] This may be another hint that Mark's Gospel is composed with Gentile readers in mind. At any rate, the principle that divorce initiated by wives counts as adultery if followed by remarriage shows that Jesus' teaching about the permanence of marriage applies to both men and women, however their marriage is contracted.

At first glance, verse 11 seems to be just repeating the familiar point that remarriage after divorce is adultery. "Whoever divorces his wife and marries another commits adultery against her." But the addition of two words "against her" is very significant. As we have seen, traditionally adultery was viewed as an offense against the husband not against the wife. So if a man divorced his wife and then married another divorced woman, he committed adultery against the second woman's first husband. It was not an offense against his first wife. But Jesus now says it *is* adultery. So here we have adultery redefined as infidelity by either party in a marriage. The old understanding was that infidelity by the wife was adulterous and an offense against her husband and the other man. But Jesus now includes the first wife as offended against if her husband divorces her and remarries another. This abrogates the double standard and represents a notable step towards women's equality.

The account of the debate with the Pharisees in the Gospel of Mark presents the issues in a slightly simplified way perhaps because the Gospel is designed for readers unfamiliar with Jewish law on marriage. It does not contradict the similar account in Matthew. Though it does not mention the exception clause, it presupposes the requirement in both Jewish and Roman law that wives guilty of adultery must be divorced. This requirement,

---

2. Amram, *Jewish Law of Divorce*, 61.

when coupled with the principle that to marry a divorcee is adultery, leads to the conclusion expressed by the exception clause in Matthew 5 and 19. Thus, there is no difference between the no-re-marriage stance in Mark and the position declared in Matthew.

However, Mark does develop the first Gospel's principles in important ways. He deals with the situation where the wife divorces her husband, a rarity in first-century Palestine but more common elsewhere in the Roman Empire. The woman who divorces and remarries is just as guilty of adultery as a man who divorces and remarries, Jesus declares.

Jesus in Mark also redefines adultery when he says that a man who divorces and remarries commits adultery against her. Previously, Jews, like most ancient peoples, held that a husband's infidelity was a sin against the other party's family, not against his own wife. Thus a woman was expected to be totally loyal to her husband, but he was allowed more license. This, the double standard, was abolished by Jesus.

LUKE 16:18

"Everyone who divorces his wife and marries another commits adultery, and he who marries a woman divorced from her husband commits adultery" is the only verse in Luke to deal with divorce and remarriage. The first half of the verse, "Everyone who divorces his wife and marries another commits adultery," corresponds to Mark 10:11, "Whoever divorces his wife and marries another commits adultery against her"; while the second half, "and he who marries a woman divorced from her husband commits adultery," corresponds to Matthew 5:32, "Whoever marries a divorced woman commits adultery." That is not to say Luke's version of Jesus teaching has been created by amalgamating Matthew and Mark's versions. In fact, Gospel scholars tend to regard Luke 16:18 as probably the closest to Jesus' exact wording as it passes the basic form-critical tests for authenticity very easily.

While it is relatively easy to defend the originality of this version of Jesus' teaching, it is not so easy to explain its position in chapter 16 of Luke. It is preceded and followed by a series of sayings and parables mostly about wealth—the unjust steward (16:1–12); God and money (16:13); Pharisees and money (16:14–15); and the rich man and Lazarus (16:19–31). After criticizing the attitude of the Pharisees toward money, Jesus says: "Everyone who divorces his wife and marries another commits adultery, and he who marries a woman divorced from her husband commits adultery" (Luke 16:18).

This saying is immediately preceded by a comment on the permanent validity of the law: "It is easier for heaven and earth to pass away than one dot of the law to become void." To "become void" is an interpretation of "pass away." "Luke, like other ancient historians, insists that the ancient laws must be kept, not abolished." Even when change in the law occurred (e.g., admission of Gentiles at the Council of Jerusalem in Acts 15), "Luke must insist that this was the original intention of the ancient laws, and therefore constitutes no change."[3] In other words, this verse is making the same point as Matthew 19:4–8, where Jesus declares that his abrogation of the Mosaic divorce law is consonant with God's original intention in creating mankind in two sexes.

> He answered, "Have you not read that he who created them from the beginning made them male and female," and said, "Therefore a man shall leave his father and his mother and hold fast to his wife, and the two shall become

---

3. David L. Balch, "Acts," in *Eerdmans Commentary on the Bible*, ed. James D. G. Dunn and John W. Rogerson (Grand Rapids: Eerdmans, 2003), 1139.

one flesh? So they are no longer two but one flesh. What therefore God has joined together, let not man separate." They said to him, "Why then did Moses command one to give a certificate of divorce and to send her away?" He said to them, "Because of your hardness of heart Moses allowed you to divorce your wives, but from the beginning it was not so." (Matt 19:4–8 // Mark 10:3–8)

This insistence on the permanent validity of the law echoes Matthew 5:17–19: "Do not think that I have come to abolish the Law or the Prophets; I have not come to abolish them but to fulfil them. For truly, I say to you, until heaven and earth pass away, not an iota, not a dot, will pass from the Law until all is accomplished." This passage introduces the antitheses, which include Matthew 5:31–32, the summary of Jesus' divorce teaching.

SUMMARY

It appears that all three Synoptic Gospels regard assent to Jesus' teaching on marriage and divorce as proof of loyalty to the law. There is thus no conflict between the different Gospels on how Jesus' teaching should be interpreted. All agree that divorce is contrary to the Creator's intention and that remarriage after divorce constitutes adultery, even if the law of Moses or Rome requires divorce for sexual immorality. This reading is confirmed by Luke 16:19–31, the parable of the rich man and Lazarus, whose punch line is: "If they do not hear Moses and the Prophets, neither will they be convinced if someone should rise from the dead." In other words, obedience to Christ's teaching on marriage is as fundamental as adherence to the Old Testament law.

8.
—
PAUL ON JESUS AND DIVORCE

In two of his epistles, Paul discusses marriage and divorce. His remarks are especially interesting for two reasons: first, because Paul's epistles are some of the earliest parts of the New Testament. Romans and 1 Corinthians are dated in the 50s AD, which is barely twenty-five years after Jesus' ministry, and by some estimates about thirty years before the composition of Matthew and Luke. So it is often surmised that in Paul's epistles we have the oldest and most authentic version of Jesus' teaching on divorce and remarriage.

The second very interesting feature of the divorce teaching is that Paul explicitly distinguishes between the teaching of Jesus and his own. First Corinthians 7:10 is one of four places in the epistle where he does this, but first we will look at Romans.

ROMANS 7:1–3

In Romans, Paul is not refuting heretical views current in Rome but setting out basic theological and ethical principles. Paul's teaching in Romans 7:1–3 is quite straightforward: no second marriage unless the woman remarrying is a widow:

> Or do you not know, brothers—for I am speaking to those who know the law—that the law is binding on a person only as long as he lives? For a married woman is bound by law to her husband while he lives, but if her husband dies she is released from the law of marriage. Accordingly, she will be called an adulteress if she lives with another man while her husband is alive. But if her husband dies, she is

free from that law, and if she marries another man she is not an adulteress.

There has been much discussion about which law Paul is referring to in verse 1, and no consensus has been reached. But the most natural way to understand the law is as a reference to the principles enunciated in the Gospels, that remarriage after divorce counts as adultery. That he does not have to elaborate on this "law" but just assumes it, shows that these principles were well-known and accepted in the Roman church. They were also well-known in the church at Corinth and presumably in the other churches Paul founded in the Peloponnese.

1 CORINTHIANS 7

First Corinthians 7 is one of the longest discussions of the ethics of marriage in the Bible and raises many tricky questions, some of which were addressed in *Jesus and Divorce.* It is not my purpose to reopen them here, but simply to focus on Paul's specific remarks about divorce in 1 Corinthians 7:8–16.

Paul had received a letter from Corinth which raised a number of issues ranging from food offered to idols to the resurrection of the dead. One of these topics concerned how to behave in the marriage relationship, "Now concerning the matters about which you wrote: 'It is good for a man not to have sexual relations with a woman'" (1 Cor 7:1). This opens a long refutation of the Corinthian view that sexual abstinence is desirable in marriage. Paul puts it bluntly: "Do not deprive one another, except perhaps by agreement for a limited time" (7:5).

Paul then goes on to discuss the more complicated issues facing single persons and those contemplating divorce. Here he is equally direct. In verses 10–11, he states what the Lord (Jesus) commanded: wives must not divorce their husbands, and husbands must not divorce their wives. If for some unstated reason divorce cannot be avoided, there are only two options for the wife, either to remain single or to be reconciled.

> To the married I give this charge (not I, but the Lord): the wife should not separate from her husband (but if she does, she should remain unmarried or else be reconciled to her husband), and the husband should not divorce his wife. (1 Cor 7:10–11)

This is a straightforward summary of the implications of the Gospel sayings. It differs only in prioritizing divorce initiated by the wife, something that was rare in the Jewish context but commonplace in Greek and Roman society (compare Mark 10:12). There is no mention of remarriage after divorce; on the contrary, it is explicitly excluded (verse 11). Nor is there any mention of mandatory divorce for sexual immorality, though verse 11 could apply to this type of situation. Like Jesus in Matthew 19:10–12, Paul expects both parties to a divorce to remain single after divorce.

He then proceeds to deal with another issue raised by the letter sent to Paul by the Corinthians. Some of them evidently went further than just abstaining from sex with their spouses and thought that if their spouse was not a believer, he or she should be divorced. Paul prefaces his remarks by mentioning that on this issue he is giving his own opinion not passing on a command of the Lord.

> To the rest I say (I, not the Lord) that if any brother has a wife who is an unbeliever, and she consents to live with him, he should not divorce her. If any woman has a husband who is an unbeliever, and he consents to live with her, she should not divorce him. For the unbelieving husband

is made holy because of his wife, and the unbelieving wife is made holy because of her husband. Otherwise your children would be unclean, but as it is, they are holy. But if the unbelieving partner separates, let it be so. In such cases the brother or sister is not enslaved. God has called you to peace. For how do you know, wife, whether you will save your husband? Or how do you know, husband, whether you will save your wife? (1 Cor 7:12–16)

On this optimistic note, Paul ends his directions about divorce.[1]

SUMMARY

Paul is often alleged to go further than Jesus in allowing divorce not just for sexual immorality but for desertion by a non-believing spouse. This is a misreading of 1 Corinthians 7:10–16. In saying the believer is not bound or "enslaved," Paul is simply allowing the believer to agree to an unbeliever's insistent demand for divorce—that is, the believer is not bound by Christ's prohibition of divorce since the responsibility lies on the unbeliever. Here Paul cites a word of Jesus which demands either reconciliation or singleness if couples separate; remarriage does not come into the picture. His overriding goal is unity in a peaceful marriage, so he discusses only these possibilities. After dealing with other issues peculiar to the Corinthian situation, he sums up his conclusion in much the same way as Romans 7:1–3: "A wife is bound to her husband as long as he lives. But if her husband dies, she is free to be married to whom she wishes, only in the Lord."

Thus Paul reiterates his conviction that a second marriage is only permitted for the believer if their first spouse has died.

---

1. For alternative interpretations, see William A. Heth and Gordon J. Wenham, *Jesus and Divorce* (London: Hodder & Stoughton, 1984), 140–44.

9.

THE OLDEST INTERPRETERS OF THE GOSPEL DIVORCE TEXTS

All Bible readers are aware to a greater or lesser extent of the danger of reading their own ideas into the text—that is, eisegesis—rather than bringing out the author's intended meaning, which is exegesis. The danger is particularly present when topics of such universal concern as marriage and divorce are discussed. That is why in the previous chapters we have spent so much time explaining marriage customs and divorce laws in the ancient world, which form the background to the biblical texts. By doing this I hope to retrieve the original context of Jesus' teaching and reduce the pressure of twenty-first-century prejudices in interpreting that teaching. Albert Schweitzer, a rather radical Bible critic, said that the problem with many scholarly portraits of Jesus was that they were like someone looking down a well and seeing a face at the bottom and supposing it was the face of Jesus, when of course it was a reflection of the scholar himself.[1] We want to avoid that pitfall here. We want to recover the real teaching of Jesus about marriage, not our own prejudices masquerading as truth.

There is another approach to avoiding this danger of eisegesis. Instead of looking back at the prehistory of the texts, one can look forward at how they were understood by later interpreters. And it seems likely that the closer the interpreter is to the original time and setting of the text, the more likely he is to understand the author's intention. This is particularly probable where the text is

1. Gordon J. Wenham, "The Face at the Bottom of the Well," in *He Swore an Oath: Biblical Themes from Genesis 12–50*, ed. Richard S. Hess, Gordon J. Wenham, and Philip E. Satterthwaite, 2nd ed. (Grand Rapids: Baker, 1994), 185–209.

a quasi-official one such as the Gospels, especially a text with large implications for the daily life of many readers and backed by oral tradition. In the early church, new converts would be expected to memorize texts from the Gospels.[2] Their authority would be confirmed from time to time when Christian leaders who knew the apostles came and taught the outlying churches.[3] It is thus intrinsically likely that in the first and second Christian centuries, the teaching of Jesus on marriage would have been known and taught by those who themselves had been taught by the apostles. This makes their writings of special value for the interpretation of the New Testament.

Catholics have long recognized this, but modern Protestants tend to need reminding that this was also the view of the Reformers. Educated by leading teachers of the Renaissance, the Reformers repeatedly claimed that they were not arguing for innovation in the church but for a return to the beliefs and practices of the early church. Martin Bucer, the Strasbourg reformer, called for "the highest esteem and singular reverence" to be paid to what these early Christian writers taught and practiced.[4] In his *Apology of the Church of England*, John Jewel wrote that the Reformed Church has "returned again unto the primitive church of the ancient fathers and apostles."[5] Similarly, John Calvin quotes abundantly from these early writers, saying, "I could with

2. Paul J. Griffiths, *Religious Reading* (New York: Oxford University Press, 1999); David M. Carr, *Writing on the Tablet of the Heart* (New York: Oxford University Press, 2005).

3. Richard Bauckham, *Jesus and the Eyewitnesses: The Gospels as Eyewitness Testimony,* 2nd ed. (Grand Rapids: Eerdmans, 2017).

4. D. F. Wright, ed., *Common Places of Martin Bucer*, Courtenay Library of Reformation Classics 4 (Abingdon: Sutton Courtenay, 1972), 41.

5. John Jewel, *The Apology of the Church of England,* ed. Richard W. Jelf, trans. Anne Lady Bacon (London: Society for Promoting Christian Knowledge, 1849), 152.

no trouble at all prove that the greater part of what we are saying today meets their approval."[6] As heirs of the Reformation, today's Protestants should recover a respect for the opinions of the early church fathers. To this end, I shall summarize some of the key passages in the works of the first two centuries: only time and space prevents us looking at the teaching of these early Christian theologians in the subsequent centuries. This would not change our conclusions, just deepen them.[7]

SHEPHERD OF HERMAS

We begin with the *Shepherd of Hermas,* a text that was very highly regarded in the early church. Some, such as Irenaeus, Clement of Alexandria, and Tertullian, indeed argued that it should be included in Scripture. It dates from immediately after the apostolic era, that is, somewhere between AD 100 and 150.[8] On conventional datings of the Gospels (c. AD 70–90) this is barely a couple of decades after the last Gospels were written. Thus, at the very least, *Hermas* gives us a picture of the marriage discipline of the church in Rome at this time. The primary issue *Hermas* addresses in relation to marriage is: What should be done when a believer or his wife commits adultery and then the guilty party repents? Can the marriage be restored? In a dialogue between Hermas and an angel, Hermas asks the angel:

> 1[29]:4 I say to him, "Sir, permit me to ask thee a few more questions." "Say on," saith he. "Sir," say I, "if a man who

---

6. John Calvin, *Institutes of the Christian Religion,* ed. John T. McNeill, trans. Ford Lewis Battles (Louisville, KY: Westminster John Knox Press, 2011), 18.

7. For a full and definitive study, see H. Crouzel, *L'Église primitive face au divorce.*

8. It has even been dated to the first century AD.

has a wife that is faithful in the Lord detect her in adultery, doth the husband sin in living with her?"

1[29]:5 "So long as he is ignorant," saith he, "he sinneth not; but if the husband know of her sin, and the wife repent not, but continue in her fornication, and her husband live with her, he makes himself responsible for her sin and an accomplice in her adultery." [9]

Roman law insisted that an unfaithful wife should be divorced within sixty days, and this may lie behind this question, but no time limit is prescribed here as long as the husband is unaware of his wife's infidelity. But when he realizes her sin, he must divorce her.

Hermas continues:

1[29]:6 "What then, Sir," say I, "shall the husband do, if the wife continue in this case?" "Let him divorce her," saith he, "and let the husband abide alone: but if after divorcing his wife he shall marry another, he likewise committeth adultery."

Not only must the husband divorce his unfaithful wife, he must remain single. If he remarries, he commits adultery. Remarriage would also prevent reconciliation between the parties if the adulteress repents.

1[29]:7 "If then, Sir," say I, "after the wife is divorced, she repent and desire to return to her own husband, shall she not be received?"

---

9. This and the following translations are from J. B. Lightfoot, *The Apostolic Fathers* (London: Macmillan and Co., 1891), 424.

1[29]:8 "Certainly," saith he, "if the husband receiveth her not, he sinneth and bringeth great sin upon himself; nay, one who hath sinned and repented must be received, yet not often; for there is but one repentance for the servants of God. For the sake of her repentance therefore the husband ought not to marry. This is the manner of acting enjoined on husband and wife."

These instructions follow those of Matthew's Gospel quite precisely. *Hermas* allows for no remarriage by the husband after he has divorced her, just like Matthew, Mark, and Luke. Like Matthew, *Hermas* requires a wife guilty of adultery to be divorced as long as she persists in her sin. The Gospel divorce texts do not deal with what should be done if she repents, though the immediate previous teaching in Matthew 18 is about the duty of forgiveness. Jesus requires seventy-sevenfold forgiveness (Matt 18:22), whereas *Hermas* limits it to just one time. Doubtless Jesus' words are hyperbole, but *Hermas* does seem to eviscerate their challenge by allowing repentant sinners only one chance.

Nevertheless, *Hermas* shows that a strict rule on divorce was maintained in his circles in Rome. These included his brother Pius, the bishop of Rome. Since *Shepherd of Hermas* was one of the most popular Christian books in the second and third centuries AD, it therefore constitutes a strong witness to the views on divorce and remarriage most common in the early church.

JUSTIN MARTYR

Another highly respected writer in the second century was Justin Martyr. Converted in about AD 130, he became a fearless defender of the faith until he was beheaded in about AD 165 for refusing to worship the emperor. His written works include a *First* and

Second Apology and a *Dialogue with Trypho*, which is a debate with a Jew about the fulfillment of Old Testament prophecy. Chapter 15 of his *First Apology* contains a brief summary of Jesus' teaching on marriage:

> He uttered such sentiments as these: "Whosoever looks upon a woman to lust after her, has committed adultery with her already in his heart before God." And, "If your right eye offend you, cut it out; for it is better for you to enter into the kingdom of heaven with one eye, than, having two eyes, to be cast into everlasting fire." And, "Whosoever shall marry her that is divorced from another husband, commits adultery." And, "There are some who have been made eunuchs of men, and some who were born eunuchs, and some who have made themselves eunuchs for the kingdom of heaven's sake; but all cannot receive this saying." So that all who, by human law, are twice married, are in the eye of our Master sinners, and those who look upon a woman to lust after her. For not only he who in act commits adultery is rejected by Him, but also he who desires to commit adultery: since not only our works, but also our thoughts, are open before God.[10]

This is an abbreviated version of Matthew 5:22–32; 19:3–12. It includes a brief statement of the marriage discipline that he ascribes to Jesus: "All who, by human law, are twice married, are in the eye of our Master sinners." What does "twice married" mean? Various suggestions have been put forward. Bigamy is one possibility, but that is incompatible with Roman law, whereas

---

10. Adapted from Justin Martyr, "The First Apology of Justin," in *The Apostolic Fathers with Justin Martyr and Irenaeus*, ed. Alexander Roberts, James Donaldson, and A. Cleveland Coxe, vol. 1, The Ante-Nicene Fathers (Buffalo, NY: Christian Literature Company, 1885), 167.

being "twice married" is allowed by human law. Remarriage after the death of one's spouse could be regarded as being twice married, but this is not condemned in the New Testament. After careful discussion, the leading authority on remarriage in the early church concludes that twice married means "remarried after divorce."[11] This Jesus condemned as adultery. He thereby implies that the first union survived divorce, so while remarriage might have been permitted under Roman law, in the eyes of God it was adultery.

Justin, like Hermas, operated in and around Rome. Their remarks show how the Gospel texts were applied in the western Roman Empire. We shall now look at two famous churchmen of the eastern Roman Empire.

CLEMENT OF ALEXANDRIA

Little is known of the life of Clement, one of the founding fathers of the very influential school of theology based in Alexandria. He was born about AD 150, possibly in Athens, and died about AD 215. He was a convert to Christianity who had studied a variety of philosophers and religions before his conversion; his later work was heavily influenced by Plato. So his works draw on these sources more than biblical exegesis. On marriage, the Alexandrians were particularly concerned to refute the Gnostics' denigration of marriage and defend it from the charge of uncleanness.

Consequently, Clement has not left a systematic exposition of the Christian view of marriage, but various remarks show he shared the same principles as we find in Hermas and Justin. In *Stromata* 2.23, he cites Scripture as saying, "whoever receives a divorced woman commits adultery"[12] Fornication is recognized

---

11. Crouzel, *L'Église primitive face au divorce*, 53–56.
12. *Stromata* 2.23; cited in Crouzel, *L'Église primitive face au divorce*, 71.

as the only valid reason for divorce, but this does not alter the ban on second marriages that follows: "Any remarriage during the life of one's spouse is adultery," and "Whoever divorces an adulterous spouse must remain single."[13] Therefore, according to Clement, remarriage is not authorized.[14] A second marriage after the death of one's spouse is not condemned, but it is regarded as a remedy for covetousness (concupiscence).[15]

Crouzel sums up his review of Clement's teaching on this topic by saying that Clement holds firmly to the thought of the apostle (Paul), and on the wider issues he holds firmly to the teaching. Our next theologian was a pupil of Clement and one of the outstanding biblical scholars of the early church.

ORIGEN

Origen was born in Alexandria to a Christian family in about AD 185 and died in Caesarea in about AD 254. Like his older contemporary Clement, he also had a classical education. But he studied the Bible in depth as well; subsequently, his biblical scholarship fitted him for his great contributions to textual criticism and commentary writing. Greek was his mother tongue but, unusually, he also knew Hebrew. This enabled him to prepare his Hexapla, in which he set alongside the Hebrew text of the Old Testament the Greek translations, such as the Septuagint, thus making it possible to establish the original text more accurately. He also wrote many books, including commentaries on different books of the Bible. One of these commentaries was on Matthew; unfortunately, the sections on the early chapters on the Sermon on the Mount

---

13. Crouzel, *L'Église primitive face au divorce*, 71.

14. Crouzel, *L'Église primitive face au divorce*, 73.

15. Crouzel, *L'Église primitive face au divorce*, 74.

are missing. However, a commentary on chapter 19 of the Gospel and numerous sermons have survived to give us an insight into his views on marriage and divorce.

On the main points of marital ethics, he is in close agreement with the teaching of Hermas and Justin. Thus he, too, regards marriage after divorce as a form of adultery. Like them, Origen holds that it is compulsory to divorce a persistently unfaithful spouse. He says nothing about the innocent party remarrying in such cases, but in view of his close agreement with his predecessors on other points of marriage discipline, it is quite unlikely that he approved of it. This is confirmed by his attitude to a reported case of a divorced woman remarrying in Egypt, which he said the local bishops allowed although they knew it was contrary to Christ's teaching, a point he reiterates twice. The bishops allowed it, they said, to prevent worse evils. Origen does allow the widowed to remarry, though he regards it as less than ideal. He prefers them to remain single as Paul does (1 Cor 7:40).[16]

SUMMARY

We have surveyed the views of four of the leading churchmen in the first two centuries of the Christian church. Hermas and Justin Martyr were representative of the Western church and were centered on Rome, while Clement and Origen represented the Eastern church and worked in Alexandria and the Holy Land. These two wings of the world church did not always agree with each other—indeed, in 1054 they broke apart in the Great Schism. But in the first five centuries, both sides were in full agreement as to what Jesus taught about divorce and remarriage: with one anomalous exception they all agreed with Hermas, whose views

---

16. See Crouzel, *L'Église primitive face au divorce,* 74–93, for a full discussion.

were so respected that some argued for his work to be regarded as Scripture.[17]

These early writers held that to remarry after divorce was to commit adultery even if the would-be remarrier was the innocent party. They understood that the exception clause did not merely allow the innocent party to divorce their spouse but required it.

This demand shocks modern Christians who believe Jesus required unlimited forgiveness. They appeal to passages like Matthew 18:22. This is partially correct, but it is also true that Jesus taught that the church must exercise a firm discipline on recalcitrant sinners (see, for example, Matt 18:6–9; 15–20).[18] I would suggest that these rules envisage a situation where the sinner is not wavering but set on his or her adulterous path.

We have looked at the views of only four early Christian writers from the first two centuries of the post-apostolic era. However, the full and definitive study of all the Christian writers in the first five centuries comes to very similar conclusions. That study lists twenty-five writers and two early councils who rejected remarriage after divorce.[19] This consensus is remarkable, for on a great many issues the church was divided and rent by fierce controversy, including disputes over such central doctrines as

---

17. The exception is so-called Ambrosiaster, who wrote commentaries on some New Testament books c. AD 366–383. For a while he was identified with Bishop Ambrose of Milan. When that was recognized as a mistake, the name Ambrosiaster was coined to identify the author of these works. He seems to have been heavily influenced by Roman law, for besides allowing deserted divorcees and innocent husbands to remarry, he also gave more license to husbands than to wives. This contradicts 1 Cor 7:3–4, which insists on parity of conjugal rights between men and women in marriage, a principle generally accepted in the early church.

18. Other examples of severe discipline include Acts 5:1–13; 2 Cor 2:1; 7:10–12; 13:1–6.

19. Crouzel, *L'Église primitive face au divorce*, 360.

the incarnation, the Trinity, Christology, sin, redemption, and the sacraments. If ever there was a doctrine that fulfilled the Vincentian canon of orthodoxy—"what has been believed everywhere, always, and by all"[20]—the traditional teaching on divorce and remarriage fulfills it abundantly.

20.   Saint Vincent of Lérins (died c. AD 440) wrote at length on criteria for distinguishing heresy from orthodoxy. Fidelity to Scripture was the primary concern, but when interpreters disagreed he invoked the principle of universality: "We shall conform to the principle of universality if we confess as alone true the faith professed by the entire church throughout the world." It is summed up in the slogan, often called the Vincentian canon, that the true faith is "what has been believed everywhere, always and by all." J. N. D. Kelly, *Early Christian Doctrines* (London: A&C Black, 1960), 50.

EPILOGUE

This study has ranged far and wide over nearly three thousand years of social history in the lands of the Bible. We began by looking at marriage law and customs in the ancient Near East, which form the background to Jewish laws on marriage and divorce, which in turn are the setting for the New Testament teaching. We examined the relevant texts in their canonical order. So we looked first at Matthew 1, where Joseph proposes to divorce his bride Mary for her apparent adultery. This episode has been rather neglected in discussions of the Gospel divorce texts, but here it is argued that it demonstrates how the exception clause was supposed to operate. Under Jewish law, a man who detected his wife or fiancée in adultery had to divorce her. This is what Joseph, a righteous man, was planning to do until the angel corrected him. It is just this sort of situation that the law envisages. According to Jesus' teaching in the Sermon on the Mount, however, any kind of divorce is as serious as adultery.

Later, while debating with the Pharisees, Jesus rules out divorce "for any cause" as favored by the liberal Hillelite Pharisees. He also rejected the stance of the more conservative Shammaites: they permitted divorce only for sexual immorality but allowed the innocent party to marry again. Jesus is stricter still. He allows separation for sexual immorality but gives no permission to remarry even to the innocent party. The disciples protested that this was too severe: it would be better not to marry than to be tied permanently to a potentially unfaithful woman.

It is important to underline that I think Jesus does not allow divorce; he permits only separation. This is clearest in Paul's summary of Jesus' teaching, but it is also the clear implication of the Gospels, which all condemn marriage after divorce as adultery. So Jesus does not agree with Shammai, the strictest rabbi, who did allow marriage in cases of divorce for adultery. The key clause in any Jewish divorce certificate, including a Shammaite one, is "You are free to marry any man." Without such a declaration, the divorce is not valid. So I do not think my view can be accused of equating Jesus' teaching with Shammai's. The early church (see the *Shepherd of Hermas*) pointed out that allowing separation but not divorce kept the possibility of reconciliation open, whereas if divorce with the right of remarriage is permitted, it probably excludes reconciliation. This is in line with Paul's teaching (1 Cor 7:11, 15–16).

More problematic is the New Testament demand that adulterers must be divorced or separate. But what should be done if the guilty party is intransigent and unrepentant? Should the innocent party and the church just put up with it, or should some discipline be exercised? To ignore the sin is very hard on the innocent party, and, if James Dobson is right (see his *Love Must Be Tough*), it is unlikely to lead to repentance. A firm reaction putting the sinner in the social wilderness and excluding him or her from church life could prompt second thoughts and lead to repentance if that option has not been closed by remarriage. In that welcome development, the innocent party must forgive the sinner and be reconciled.

On the other hand, if the guilty party repents, the other party must welcome the restoration of the marriage. But there should be a limit on the number of times the innocent party is expected to forgive the unfaithful spouse; while Jesus spoke of seventy-seven times, Hermas reckoned once should be the limit. After the death of one's spouse, remarriage was permissible but not recommended. The theology of their opposition to divorce and remarriage is based on Christ's appeal to Genesis 1 and 2. There Jesus traces marriage to the Creator's design so that its unity is not dissolved in a legal sense by divorce.

As usual, when listeners found his teaching too hard, Jesus did not recant; instead, he called his disciples to take up his challenge for the sake of the kingdom of heaven, that is, out of loyalty to him. Paul and the rest of the early church embraced this challenge and made "no remarriage after divorce" part of orthodox Christian teaching. But the challenge is widely forgotten in the Protestant churches today. Indeed, it is quite difficult to obtain a hearing for the no-remarriage view.

It is my hope that this traditional view will again be taken seriously by Bible commentators, Christian ethicists, clergy, and pastors. But those who are concerned to promote the no-remarriage line must proceed with the utmost tact and discretion, for there are countless sincere believers who, ignorant of the correct reading of the Gospel divorce sayings, have themselves remarried or encouraged others to marry again. They have done this in all innocence and have often been greatly blessed in their relationship or ministry. They are vivid reminders that God blesses us in spite of our failings and weaknesses, not because we are perfect. As Frederick Faber put it:

> There's a wideness in God's mercy
> Like the wideness of the sea;
> There's a kindness in his justice
> Which is more than liberty.

There is no place where earth's sorrows
Are more felt than up in heaven;
There is no place where earth's failings
Have such kindly judgment given.

For the love of God is broader
Than the measures of man's mind;
And the heart of the Eternal
Is most wonderfully kind.[1]

---

1.   Frederick W. Faber, "There's a Wideness in God's Mercy" (1862).

BIBLIOGRAPHY

Allison, Dale C. "Divorce, Celibacy and Joseph (Matthew 1:18–25 and 19:1–12)." *Journal for the Study of the New Testament* 49.1 (1993): 3–10.

Amram, David W. *The Jewish Law of Divorce according to Bible and Talmud with Some Reference to Its Development in Post-Talmudic Times.* 1896. Reprint, New York: Hermon Press, 1975.

Bockmuehl, Markus. "Matthew 5:32, 19:9 in the Light of Pre-Rabbinic Halakhah. *New Testament Studies* 35.2 (1989): 291–95.

Burnside, Jonathan. *God, Justice, and Society.* New York: Oxford University Press, 2011.

Carr, David M. *Writing on the Tablet of the Heart: Origins of Scripture and Literature.* New York: Oxford University Press, 2005.

Catchpole, David R. "The Synoptic Divorce Material as a Traditio-Historical Problem." *Bulletin of the John Rylands Library* 57 (1974): 92–127.

Craigie, Peter C. *Deuteronomy.* 2nd ed. New International Commentary on the Old Testament. Grand Rapids: Eerdmans, 1976.

Crouzel, Henri. *L'Église primitive face au divorce.* Paris: Beauchesne, 1971.

De Vaux, Roland. *Ancient Israel: Its Life and Institutions.* London: Darton, Longman, & Todd, 1962.

Dupont, Jacques. *Mariage et divorce dans l'Évangile.* Bruges: Desclée de Brouwer, 1959.

Granquist, Hilma. *Marriage Conditions in a Palestinian Village, vol. II.* Helsingfors: Akademische Buchhandlung, 1935.

Griffiths, Paul J. *Religious Reading: The Practice of Reading the Practice of Religion.* New York: Oxford University Press, 1999.

Hankore, Daniel. *The Abduction of Dinah: Reading Genesis 28:10–35:15 as a Votive Narrative*. Eugene, OR: Pickwick, 2013.

Hazony, Yoram. *The Philosophy of Hebrew Scripture*. Cambridge: Cambridge University Press, 2012.

Hess, Richard S., and M. Daniel Carroll R. *Family in the Bible: Exploring Customs, Culture, and Context*. Grand Rapids: Baker Academic, 2003.

Heth, William A., and Gordon J. Wenham. *Jesus and Divorce*. London: Hodder & Stoughton, 1984.

Hugenberger, Gordon P. *Marriage as a Covenant: Biblical Law and Ethics as Developed from Malachi*. Supplements to Vetus Testamentum 52. Leiden: Brill, 1994.

Instone-Brewer, David. *Divorce and Remarriage in the Bible*. Grand Rapids: Eerdmans, 2002.

——. *Divorce and Remarriage in the Church*. Carlisle: Paternoster, 2003.

Keil, C. F., and Franz Delitzsch. *Biblical Commentary on the Old Testament*. Reprint ed. Grand Rapids: Eerdmans, 1988.

Kelly, J. N. D. *Early Christian Doctrines*, 2nd ed. London: A&C Black, 1960.

Luz, Ulrich. *Matthew 1–7: A Commentary*. Hermeneia. Minneapolis: Fortress Press, 2007.

——. *Matthew 8–20: A Commentary*. Hermeneia. Minneapolis: Fortress Press, 2001.

Newheiser, Jim. *Marriage, Divorce, and Remarriage: Crucial Questions and Answers*. Philipsburg, NJ: P&R, 2017.

Quesnell, Quentin. "Made Themselves Eunuchs for the Kingdom of Heaven (Mt 19,12)." *Catholic Biblical Quarterly* 30 (1968): 335–58.

Parry, Robin A. *Old Testament Story and Christian Ethics:The Rape of Dinah as a Case Study*. Leicester: Inter-Varsity Press, 2004.

Roth, Martha T. *Law Collections from Mesopotamia and Asia Minor*. 2nd ed. Writings from the Ancient World 6. Atlanta: Scholars Press, 1997.

Vermes, Geza. *The Dead Sea Scrolls in English*. London: Penguin Books, 2004.

Wenham, Gordon J. "*BETULAH*: A Girl of Marriageable Age." *Vetus Testamentum* 22.3 (1972): 326–48.

——. *Exploring the Old Testament, Vol. 1: A Guide to the Pentateuch*. Downers Grove, IL: InterVarsity Press, 2003.

———. "Matthew and Divorce: An Old Crux Revisited." *Journal for the Study of the New Testament* 22 (1984): 95–107.

———. "May Divorced Christians Remarry?" *Churchman* 95 (1981): 150–61.

———. "The Restoration of Marriage Reconsidered." *Journal of Jewish Studies* 30 (1979): 36–40.

———. "The Syntax of Matthew 19:9." *Journal for the Study of the New Testament* 28 (1986): 17–23.

Westbrook, Raymond. *Old Babylonian Marriage Law*. Horn, Austria: Verlag Ferdinand Berger & Söhne, 1988.

———. *Property and the Family in Biblical Law*. Library of Hebrew Bible/Old Testament Studies. Sheffield: Sheffield Academic, 1991.

Williamson, Hugh G. M. *Ezra, Nehemiah*. Word Biblical Commentary. Waco: Word Books, 1985.

Yaron, Reuven. "Aramaic Marriage Contracts from Elephantine." *Journal of Semitic Studies* 3 (1958): 1–39.

———. "The Restoration of Marriage." *Journal of Jewish Studies* 17 (1966): 1–11.

SUBJECT INDEX

——

SCRIPTURE INDEX

—

OLD TESTAMENT